MORMON Pioneer DANCES

Mormon Pioneer Dances

31 Authentic Dances of the Early Saints

Compiled by
Laraine Miner

CFI
An Imprint of Cedar Fort, Inc.
Springville, Utah

To my aunt Aline Coleman Smith (age 105),
who pioneered the dance department at
Brigham Young University at age sixteen
and who has been my most ardent supporter.

Illustrations by David Sharp
Music transcriptions by David Sharp and Larry Shumway

ISBN 13: 978-1-4621-2049-9

Published by CFI, an imprint of Cedar Fort, Inc.
2373 W. 700 S., Springville, UT 84663
Distributed by Cedar Fort, Inc., www.cedarfort.com

LIBRARY OF CONGRESS CATALOGING-IN-PUBLICATION DATA ON FILE

Cover design by Kinsey Beckett

Edited and typeset by Rebecca Bird and Chelsea Holdaway

Printed in the United States of America

10 9 8 7 6 5 4 3 2 1

Printed on acid-free paper

Preface ix

Acknowledgments xi

Introduction 1

PART ONE: Religious, Cultural, and Historical Background of Mormon Pioneer Dances 3

PART TWO: Ten Dances for Trek Reenactments, Family Reunions, and Community Celebrations 27

The Grand March 27

The Virginia Reel 32

Haste to the Wedding 37

Oslo Waltz 40

Spanish Waltz (Over the Waves) 43

Danish Slide-Off 46

Oak City Quadrille 49

Heel-Toe Polka 56

The Patty Cake Polka 58

Five Children's Song Dances

Oh! Susanna! 63
Somebody's Waiting 66
Pop Goes the Weasel 69
Gift to Be Simple 72
All Good Children 74

More Challenging Dances

The Money Musk 77
The Tempest 80
Danish Waltz 83
Opera Reel 86
Ninepin Quadrille (Tucker Quadrille) 88
Den Toppede Høne (The Crested Hen) 92
Old Dan Tucker 94
Miss McLeod's Reel 97
Fisher's Hornpipe 99
Sir Roger de Coverley 102
Twin Sisters 106
The Scotch Reel 108
French Four 111

Archival Dances

Marlbrouk Cotillion 119
The Caledonian Quadrille 123
Plain Quadrille 128

APPENDIX A: Fiddling and Dancing unto the Lord 135

APPENDIX B: Mormon Pioneer Era Clothing for the Dance 145

Glossary 159

Resources 169

Author 177

Online Content 179

Preface

THIS PROJECT HAS grown out of my curiosity of fifty-one years. In 1964, I toured Europe with the BYU folk dancers performing American (USA) dances at folk dance festivals. For me this was a life-changing experience. Heretofore we had only performed the folk dances of other countries. Now we were performing Appalachian clogging, Kentucky running sets, and even the Native American hoop dance. It was an enormously exciting and enriching experience for me. Some audiences in remote areas had never seen Americans, let alone our traditional folk dances. So I started wondering, *What are the traditional folk/social dances of my own Mormon pioneer ancestors?* since dancing was so popular during pioneer times. This began my lifetime quest and passion of researching, collecting, teaching, and presenting these dances. I've perused libraries and museum archives all across the country. I've collaborated with folklorists and folk musicians on the same path. I've interviewed old-timers, musicians, and callers while doing field research for my master's project on early Utah dances. I've filmed a wedding and several festivals in small, rural hold-out communities where these dances are still enjoyed in living tradition. This is to name a few of my endeavors along this journey.

During this process, I've been most impressed by the way in which these dances bring people together in a "celebration of collective joy." My purpose has become "creating community and connection with dance, music, and song"—something that has dropped out of our mainstream culture, where we have become so solitary and isolated. The advancing technological world now enables us to create disembodied armchair or "virtual" relationships and connections. Yet I believe that deep down inside, we hunger for the "tribe"—a place where we are seen, heard, touched, and cared for. A place where we can feel the oneness of moving, singing, and laughing together. A place where there are talented live musicians to lift us right off our feet to express our joy. A fiddler once told me, "The greatest compliment you can give a fiddler is to dance to his music." The dances in this project are participatory dances, or "social" dances. Our modern media has unfortunately caused us to become spectators of dance, intimidated by the professionalism we see on TV and otherwise. There is an African saying, "If you can walk you can dance, if you can talk you can sing," which most certainly applies to most of these dances.

My hope is that these dances will also connect the generations. I've loved seeing families dancing together: Mom dancing as one with her toddler; Dad with the baby on his shoulders; older children dancing with their parents or grandparents. Most of all I hope these dances can bring us an appreciation and connection with our pioneer ancestors as we "dance in their shoes."

Acknowledgments

FIRST OF ALL, I wish to acknowledge and thank my two dear friends and colleagues, Michael Hamblin and Craig R. Miller, for their support, advice, and collaboration through my many years of researching and developing this project. Next I wish to thank David Millstone for his interest, urging, and invaluable feedback and expertise. I owe a debt of gratitude to Ed and Vickie Austin and Jeanette Geslison of Brigham Young University, the Pioneer Heritage Company, and the Jones family of the Eagle Mountain Family Dance group—all of whom helped make the DVD for this project. I also want to recognize and express appreciation for my collaboration with the following musicians in arranging and recording the pioneer dance music: Mark Jardine, Paul Rasmussen, Stan Jensen, and Cory Webster of the Beehive Band; Krista Baker and Dave Sharp of Idlewild Band; Mark Geslison of the Institute of American Music; and Richard Ebling of Loose Shoes Contra Dance Band.

Additionally, I wish to acknowledge the National Folk Organization and the Charles Redd Center for Western Studies, who have provided grant money to make portions of this project possible.

Last, but not least, I wish to thank and honor and thank both Mary Bee Jensen, founder of the BYU Folk dancers, and Sanna Longden, who created Pourparler, which has provided me with priceless networking opportunities and the yearly ultimate experience of collectively celebrating joy through community dancing.

Introduction

FOR THIS PROJECT, I have chosen thirty-one dances to represent the official Mormon pioneer era, from 1847 (when the pioneers arrived in the Salt Lake Valley) to 1869 (the coming of the railroad). The majority of the dances are documented in Mormon pioneer era sources. I have also attempted to tread a fine line between offering authentic dances and presenting dances agreeable to modern tastes.

The first group of ten dances is fitting for many occasions. They are especially suitable for community dancing and are appealing to all ages. They are simple and quickly taught. Teens especially love the polka.

I felt it imperative to include the five children's song dances (also know as "play parties"). They are very accessible to all ages and can be danced anytime, anywhere, since the human voice is all that is needed to accompany the dances. They are so wonderful for families and for connecting the generations.

The more challenging dances are meant for more experienced dancers who wish to delve deeper into this genre and use the dances for performance. Many are New England contra dances called "Chestnuts," a collection of old "classics" or favorites—some dating back hundreds of years, and still fondly danced today in deep New England.[1]

Of the archival dances, the Plain and Caledonian Quadrilles are authentic historical reconstructions. Quadrilles were the mainstay of the pioneers and precursors of modern square dancing. Marlbrouk Cotillion represents an older style of dance in square formation, which Brigham Young loved for its "fancy footwork." It is a fun dance for more experienced dancers to learn and enjoy.

All of the dances are accompanied by tunes from the pioneer era. The bands who play these tunes were selected for their expertise in the pioneer style. The Beehive Band in particular was chosen to represent the traditional music of the State of Utah at the Library of Congress 2006 American Folklife Homegrown Concert, where they were recorded for LOC national archives. Whenever possible, good live music is much preferable to recorded, which is why the scored tunes are included. It makes a huge difference to have live musicians who respond to the dancers and vice versa. This joyful give-and-take between musicians and dancers creates an authentic pioneer community dance experience.

I have included a chapter on pioneer era dress, since clothing always influences the style and movement of the dance. The dancing, music, and dress come together to engender the true spirit of Mormon pioneer dances.

Notes

1. David Smuckler and David Millstone, *Cracking Chestnuts* (Haydenville: Country Dance & Song Society, 2008), 7–8.

Part One

RELIGIOUS, CULTURAL, AND HISTORICAL BACKGROUND OF MORMON PIONEER DANCES

Early Beginnings
Mormonism and Puritanism

In the June 22, 1959, issue of *Time Magazine*, an article declared The Church of Jesus Christ of Latter-day Saints as the "Dancingest Denomination" due to the prevalence of dancing in the Mormon culture. At the time of the article, there was even an official calling of "dance director" in each congregation, or ward. How curious that a conservative Christian church, originating in nineteenth century Puritan New England, should be named such.

During the early days of The Church of Jesus Christ of Latter-day Saints, in Kirtland, Ohio, twenty-two members—male and female—were disfellowshipped for "uniting with the world in a dance" at a public dance hall, and threatened with excommunication if they did not repent of their "wickedness." Nevertheless, it was not the act of dancing that was decried, but the association with the worldly and base elements of a public dance hall.[1]

In 1841, after being driven out by mobs to hither and yon and threatened with an extermination order, the homeless and poverty-stricken refugee Mormons settled and built the town of Nauvoo, Illinois, on the banks of the Mississippi. Not long after Joseph Smith's Mansion House was built, weekly dancing parties were held there, with a few hundred youth participating in these Church-sponsored events. On Christmas Day in 1843, Joseph Smith recorded the following in his diary: "A large party supped at my house, and spent the evening in music, dancing, etc., in a most cheerful and friendly manner."[2]

The Prophet Joseph Smith departed from the religious leaders of his day who forbade play by participating in such sports as baseball, wrestling, ice skating, and pulling sticks. He encouraged and promoted other recreational activities such as drama, music, and dancing, when performed within the boundaries of proper deportment and associations.[3] The Mormon "repudiation of religious pessimism" by embracing play was inspired by the Book of Mormon scripture, "Men are that they might have joy"[4] and have it more abundantly, as some have added. Mormons were not only allowing dancing but advocating and sponsoring it.

Joseph Smith's Mansion House later became a hotel where weekly cotillions were held to furnish amusement for the hotel guests and provide income for the Smiths. The young Mormon women of Nauvoo were advised to strictly avoid these dances due to the unsavory and transient nature of the river folk guests. Likewise, the local public dances were taboo, but the Church-sponsored dances became very popular, though this created the following problem:

> Candlelit, formal balls became highlights of society in Nauvoo, though many Mormons, converted from austere Protestant sects that prohibited dancing, stumbled through

the steps, with unaccustomed feet. Elder Orson Hyde described the problem of his fellow apostle, Parley P. Pratt, when quadrilles and cotillions were first introduced:

> "I observed my Brother Parley standing in the figure, and he was making no motion particularly, only up and down. Says I, 'Brother Parley, why don't you move forward:' Says he, 'When I think which way I am going I forget the step, and when I think of the step, I forget which way to go.'"

To remedy such plights, the Nauvoo Dancing School held evening lessons at the Masonic Hall.[5]

The Spiritual and the Temporal

Dancing "before the Lord" and "praising and glorifying God in the dance" were common phrases in diary entries. The dancing was tempered by admonitions to avoid excess, and proper etiquette and decorum were enforced. Within these boundaries, social dancing was sanctioned and encouraged.

In Mormonism, the spiritual and the secular are closely related, and both Brigham Young and Joseph Smith maintained the temporal and physical welfare of the Saints were the bases for their spiritual welfare. In Mormonism, all aspects of life are "consecrated" to the building up of the Kingdom of God.[6]

Though dancing was never part of a Mormon worship service, it is difficult to separate music and dancing from the Mormon lifestyle. Mormonism has never been "just a Sunday religion"—it is a complete way of life. At first it was a social order, a political order, and an economic order based on the communal principles of Christianity, all of which were enhanced by community social dancing.

According to Brigham Young, "Our work, our everyday labor, our whole lives are within the scope of our religion. This is what we believe, and what we try to practice. Recreation and diversion are as necessary to our well-being as the most serious pursuits of life. If you wish to dance, dance, and you are just as prepared for prayer meeting as you were before, if you are Saints."[7]

There was a certain "religious" quality reflected in the way the Mormons danced. Their dances were opened and dismissed with prayer, and, in such prayers, the Saints were encouraged to partake of the dancing in a "manner that would be pleasing unto God." For the pioneers, dancing became an expression of joy coupled with prayers of thanksgiving, echoing the early Israelites by showing joy and thanksgiving before the Lord for the bounties of life.

The Martyrdom of the Prophet Joseph Smith and the Completion of the Temple

On June 27, 1844, the Prophet Joseph Smith was martyred at Carthage Jail. Brigham Young became the acting leader of the Church and declared this a time for cessation of "dancing or frolic, but a time of mourning and of humiliation and prayer."

When it became clear the Mormons would soon be driven from Nauvoo, they began a feverish effort to complete the Nauvoo Temple. In his January 2, 1846, journal entry, Heber C. Kimball recorded Brigham Young sanctioning dancing in the temple:

> We praise the Lord as we please. Now as to dancing in this house . . . there are thousands of brethren and sisters that have labored to build these walls and put on this roof, and they are shut out any opportunity of enjoyment, among the wicked or in the world, and shall they have any recreations? Yes! And this is the very place where they can have liberty.[8]

There are several accounts of social dancing in the Nauvoo Temple such as this one in William Clayton's journal:

> The labors of the day having been brought to a close at so early an hour, half past 8, it was thought proper to have a little season of recreation, accordingly, Brother Hans Hanson was invited to produce his violin. He did so, and played several

> lively airs, among the rest some very good and lively dance tunes. This was too much for the gravity of Brother Joseph Young, who indulged in a hornpipe, and was soon joined by several others, and before the dance was over several French fours were indulged in. The first was opened by President B. Young with Sister Whitney and Elder H. C. Kimball with Sister Lewis. The spirit of the dancing increased until the whole floor was covered with dancers.[9]

Eventually the dancing in the temple may have become a little too boisterous, since Brigham Young later advised that "all dancing and merriment in the Temple should cease, lest they be carried away by the spirit of levity . . . that the name of Deity should be held in reverence, with all due deference that belongeth to an infinite being of his character"[10]

The Pioneer Trek

The Nauvoo Expulsion

In the mid-winter of 1846, the Mormons were driven from Nauvoo by mobbers who burned the Saints' homes and crops. The Saints were forced to flee across the Mississippi River ice in their wagons and set up camp seven miles away at Sugar Creek where Brigham Young declared this was "a time to dance!"

> The night of March 1, (1846) after they had pitched camp in the usual manner of emigrants, President Young had the "brethren and sisters" out in a dance to the tune of Captain Pitt's Brass Band. A dance! How could they? Indeed the Iowans who gathered round could scarcely believe their eyes. The men cleared away the snow in a sheltered place. Warmed and lighted by the blzing *[sic]* logs of their fire, fifty couples, old and young, stepped out in the dance.[11]

Thus, dancing provided a relief and a distraction from the mass suffering for homes burned, possessions left behind, loved ones killed, and later for those who died along the trail.

Dancing across the Plains

The Mormon pioneers crossed Iowa and camped at Winter Quarters on the banks of the Missouri River. Many of the Saints were grieving lost loved ones; others were cold, hungry, or ill. Morale was very low. Once again Brigham Young called for dancing. A fire was built near the bowery, and President Brigham summoned his people together to say, "I want you to sing and dance and forget your troubles. . . . We must think of the future that lies ahead and the work which is ours. We are to build the Kingdom of God in a new Zion. Let's have some music and all of you dance."[12] So they danced waltzes, polkas, and quadrilles to William Pitt's Brass Band. Hyrum Gates became the "dancing master" at Winter Quarters with a total of four hundred students in his dance classes that were held on weekdays from 10:00 a.m. to 3:00 p.m. and from 4:00 p.m. to 9:00 p.m.[13]

It was at Winter Quarters that Brigham Young received the following revelation recorded in Doctrine and Covenants 136:28: "If thou art merry, praise the Lord with singing, with music, with dancing, and with a prayer of praise and thanksgiving." This officially sanctioned and encouraged music and dancing for the pioneers. It became indispensable as a morale builder, a relief from trials and oppression, a way to keep warm, and relaxation from hard work—all so essential for the long and difficult journey ahead. Thereafter, each company that crossed the plains would often—after walking fifteen miles during the day—set up camp, eat, sing songs, and dance,[14] as in this colorful description:

> After another song, as if by magic a long-haired fiddler appears. The crowd clears a circle around him. A loud-voiced caller takes his place. Couples walk out and the music begins. The quadrilles, the reels of long ago, danced with many an enthusiastic fling, are started. Out on the bare ground with the clear sky overhead and the friendly glow of the camp-

> fire all about, the dancers enter into the spirit of it as only Mormon dancers can. The young, the middle aged, even the old, all catch the contagion of it. The fiddler plays with might and main, the caller shouts until he is hoarse, the dust rises in a cloud from the parched ground, but still they dance. Out on the plains, a thousand miles from civilization, in the dangerous Indian country, going, they scarcely knew where, instead of idle moaning, and the bootless thinking of the dark thoughts, they sing and they dance. When the bugle calls them to their beds, they are ready for healthful sleep.[14]

Dancing at night was frequent, but not the rule, except in the Henry W. Miller wagon company, where the activities of singing and dancing to rejuvenate their spirits were declared mandatory. A couple from Wales, John and Ellen Crofts, were assigned to gather folks up for these nightly events. One day in October 1862, Ellen Crofts recorded in her diary that they had pled the case for one couple to be excused from the festivities who had just that day buried their baby. The wagon master excused them for one night only.[15]

The Mormon Battalion Farewell Ball

In 1846, five hundred men were recruited from the Mormon pioneer refugees to serve the United States military as the "Mormon Battalion." Their orders were to march to California and assist with the Mexican-American War. The Mormon refugees had barely assembled their camps at Winter Quarters near Council Bluffs, Iowa—where Colonel Thomas Kane, friend of the Mormons, penned the following description of the Farewell Ball honoring the Battalion's July departure:

> A more merry dancing rout I have never seen. . . . It was the custom, whenever the larger camps rested for a few days together to make great arbors, or 'bowries' as they called them, of poles and brush. . . . In one of these where the ground had been trodden firm and hard . . . was gathered now the mirth and beauty of the Mormon Israel. . . . With

> the rest, attended the Elders of the Church within call, including nearly all the chiefs of the High Council, with their wives and children. They, the gravest and most trouble-worn, seemed the most anxious of any to be the first to throw off the burden of heavy thoughts. Their leading off the dancing in a great double cotillion was the signal bade the festivity commence. To the canto of debonair violins, the cheer of horns, the jingle of sleigh-bells, and the jovial snoring of the tambourine, they did dance![16]

The next morning, the five hundred men of the Mormon Battalion marched out of the encampment singing, "The Girl I Left Behind."

Colonization Period

When the Mormon pioneers began settling the Salt Lake Valley, dancing schools, taught by dancing masters, cropped up all over the valley.[17] In the winter of 1854, there were dancing schools in almost every one of the nineteen schoolhouses. According to apostate, John Hyde, "The Mormons love dancing. Almost every third man is a fiddler, and everyone must learn to dance."[18] A British traveler, Richard Burton, passing through Salt Lake City observed, "Dancing seems to be considered an edifying exercise. The Prophet dances, the Apostles dance, the Bishops dance."[19]

Colonizing the Provisional State of Deseret

After the Mormon pioneers settled the Salt Lake Valley, they proceeded to set up a government that would be recognized by the United States. Brigham Young made a proposal to establish the State of Deseret. (The term "deseret" is the Book of Mormon word for honeybee.) The Utah State symbol is a beehive representing the "perfect social order," in which everyone industriously works together in harmony. The provisional State of Deseret would have encompassed all of present-day Utah and Nevada, large portions of southern California and northern

Arizona, eastern Colorado, and adjacent parts of New Mexico, Wyoming, Idaho, and Oregon (a big and bold plan). In 1851, as a compromise, this large area was collapsed down to encompass Nevada, Utah, and Western Colorado, and declared Utah Territory by Act of Congress with Brigham Young as governor.

The concept of the "State of Deseret" still retained by the Latter-day Saints, Brigham Young continued to send out groups of Saints to colonize this larger region. Along with such craftsmen as carpenters and blacksmiths, Brigham Young made sure each town had a decent set of musicians since "dancing became almost one of the ordinances."[20]

The nineteenth century has been referred to as "The Golden Age of Social Dancing." These particular forms of social dancing, quadrilles, circles, and longways sets, were well suited for community building and creating group cohesion. In fact, Brigham Young is said to have created a formation dance he named "The Beehive Dance" for the purpose of training everyone to work together, since each person had to perform their part correctly in order for the dance to successfully work.

Recreational Relief from Hard Work

Brigham Young stated,

> I want it distinctly understood that fiddling and dancing are no part of our worship. The question may be asked, What are they for, then? I answer, that my body may keep pace with my mind. My mind labors like a man logging, all the time: and this is the reason why I am fond of these pastimes—they give me a privilege to throw everything off, and shake myself, that my body may exercise, and my mind rest. What for? To get strength and be renewed and quickened and enlivened and animated, so that my mind may not wear out.[21]

This would ring true for hard physical work as well and served this function in crossing the plains. It also took a great deal of hard physical work to create towns and communities. When the Mormon pioneers came to Zion, they entered a desert, a most inhospitable land, with only 3.3 percent arable land, and, in some areas, only 1 percent.[22] The most successful way of settling this formidable frontier was to establish communal villages, with everyone sharing in the wealth and working together in a close, mutually supportive way. Once again, high morale and good feelings were necessary to facilitate this kind of teamwork. Once again, dancing, having become the Mormon pioneers' favorite form of recreation, made a significant contribution to the morale and good feelings in the newly settled colonies.

Assimilating Immigrant Converts

From the very beginning of the Church, missionaries were sent throughout North America, Canada, and Europe. Thousands of converts immigrated to Zion, primarily from the British Isles and Scandinavia, bringing their language, culture, and traditions with them. Between 1850 and 1875, over thirty thousand Danish converts had immigrated to Utah, composing the second largest immigrant group. Dancing was a useful means for assimilating these diverse cultures, particularly for the Scandinavians. The universal language of dance provided an easy way for them to socialize, the frictions caused by language barriers dissolving when the folks were having a great time dancing together.[23]

> In 1862, John, a Danish convert, left Denmark to come to America. John was twenty-two when he and his parents settled in the small rural town of Manti, Utah, where he worked on his father's farm. John was learning English, but struggled to communicate with peers, and consequently his social life was quite lacking. Dating girls was out of the question since he didn't understand the language. So John spent his lonely free time practicing his father's accordion and taking a few flute lessons.

In Europe, the waltz was quite the fashion, but folks in Manti were just becoming aware of it. When the youth of the town found out John had learned the waltz at school in Denmark, they requested he start a waltzing school, dancing being their main form of recreation. John hesitated at first due to his difficulty with English. Then Brother Nielsen, the town schoolmaster, volunteered to be his interpreter. The waltzing school was quite successful, and John later expressed that he now felt "it was good to be in Zion."[24]

The Round Dance Controversy

The couple turning waltz originated in central Europe and was introduced to the American ballroom in the early 1800s. It soon became wildly popular, and, at the same time, very controversial. Across the nation, clergy and laity alike railed against it, calling it scandalous because a woman and a man were coupled in an embrace (closed ballroom position) while turning languidly around the dance floor. This was thought vulgar, and in poor taste due to too much "familiarity." Its steps were simple and easily learned, eliminating the need for a dancing master to teach the complexities of steps and formations along with proper deportment and manners. Some went so far as calling the waltz the "dance of death," and believed it left young women vulnerable to seduction. On the other hand, due to its widespread popularity, the waltz was eventually deemed "The Queen of the Nineteenth Century Ballroom."

Around the middle of the nineteenth century, the polka, another round dance, was introduced. Like the waltz, the polka spread like wildfire across Europe and the emerging American nation. To many of the puritanical tradition and purveyors of social etiquette and courtly refinement, this was the final affront. Dancing masters denounced the polka. In fact, it was forbidden to be danced in the presence of Queen Victoria. It was described as, "A kind of insane Tartar jig performed to disagreeable music of an uncivilized character."[25] More round dances followed such as the schottische and mazurka.

These round dances, couple waltz, polka, schottische, mazurka, and so on, were a radical departure from the more traditionally formalized set dances such as the quadrilles and longways sets, where movements were strictly prescribed. Round dance couples, in closed ballroom position, whirled randomly around the floor, independent of any prescribed form (except for the specific waltz, polka, schottische, and mazurka steps), thus threatening the proper decorum of the ballroom.

Another problem with round dancing was the close proximity between partners. My paternal grandfather, George Miner, once reminisced, "I remember when we couldn't waltz. We had to square dance. Then when we could waltz, floor mangers went around with a ruler to make sure we were the proper distance apart."

Brigham Young, along with other LDS Church leaders, initially disapproved of round dances and tried to eliminate them from Church-sponsored dances. There were two problems with this attempt. First, there were so many European, especially Scandinavian, immigrant converts who had round danced all their lives in the old country. Second, the youth of the Church, who were greatly attracted to round dancing, were insisting on their right to dance this latest fashion. Consequently, Brigham Young espoused a policy that every Church-sponsored dance in the territory should have at least some round dances, so the immigrants and youth might avoid lure of public dances. It wasn't until 1913 that the round dances became fully sanctioned at Church dances.

Mormon Battalion Farewell Ball July 1846 was held under a bowery, constructed of "poles and brush." Boweries were the first dance venues constructed in the early Mormon settlements. (Painting by CCA Christensen, copyright Intellectual Reserve, Inc. Courtesy Church History Museum.)

WHERE, WHEN, WHAT, HOW, AND WHY THEY DANCED

Where They Danced

The pioneers first danced in log cabins or barns on dirt floors. They danced barefoot to save what shoes they had. When rough pine floors were installed, they continued to dance barefoot since their feet had developed large, hard callouses impervious to slivers. They eventually used candle wax, soap, or cornstarch on the floors to make them smooth. Later they would often build an outdoor "bowery"—an arbor made of poles supporting a roof of boughs and bushes—where they held community meetings and dances. As towns became more established, the people would hold dances in the schoolhouse. Some towns went on to build social halls with a dance floor and stage for dramatic performances.

Dance parties were also held in homes where they would often empty them of furniture and then dance through the rooms and sometimes outside under the stars. When the home

Historic Fairfield District Schoolhouse in Utah was built in 1898, two years after Utah Statehood. Schoolhouses were primary venues for the more established early Mormon settlements.

The Social Hall in Salt Lake City was dedicated on Saturday, January 1, 1853. A grand ball was held there that evening with invitations issued by Brigham Young. Many balls and dramatic presentations were subsequently held in this splendid old structure. (Painting by Cornelius Salisbury, courtesy of The Daughters of Utah Pioneers' Salt Lake City Pioneer Memorial Museum.)

space became too crowded, participants were given numbers (odds and evens) to rotate in and out of the dancing.

When church meetinghouses were built, the people held dances in the recreation hall next to the chapel. If early American clergy looked askance upon the pastime of dancing, they must have found the Mormon custom of building a dance hall onto the chapel as positively scandalous.

When They Danced

Spring, summer, and fall were filled with work, so the Saints danced mostly in winter to socialize and keep warm. Dancing was also considered necessary to make most all celebrations complete.[26] These occasions included the Governor's Ball, Independence Day, Pioneer Day (July 24), Christmas, New Years, Thanksgiving, barn raisings, harvests, and so on. Each new pioneer company entering the valley was greeted and celebrated with music and dancing.

First Harvest Thanksgiving Celebration and Dance 1848:

A celebration was held in thanksgiving for the harvest of the first crops in the Salt Lake Valley, which were saved by the miracle of the seagulls from that year's massive infestation of grasshoppers. Parley P. Pratt reported the following in a letter to his brother Orson: "On the tenth of August last, we met to the number of several hundreds under a large awning to celebrate our first harvest in the Great Basin. We had a feast which consisted of a variety of foods, all produced in the valley. We had a prayer and thanksgiving, music and dancing and firing of cannon."[27]

Christmas 1852:

> When the Social Hall was completed . . . Christmas was celebrated there with dancing parties, both for the adults and children. Our girls and boys will never forget the first Christmas tree there where there was a present for every child

of several large families, and all numbered and arranged in perfect order of name and age. President Young—Brother Brigham—was foremost in making the affair a grand success. Hon. John W. Young, then only a boy, handed the present[s] down from the tree, and I recollected Brother Brigham standing and pointing with his cane, and telling John, just which to take down, and so on; the children were wild with delight and some of the mothers quite as much elated, though not as demonstrative. After the Santa Claus tree was stripped of its gifts, the floor was cleared and the dancing commenced, and there was good music too, and President Young led the dance, and "cut the pigeon wing," to the great delight of the little folks.[28]

New Year's Day 1853:

The New Year of 1853 was danced in with extra ceremony; more candles were furnished and another fiddler, William Smith, procured. All the good clothes were brought out for the occasion. Some who were mere lads at that time wearing their first breeches, can remember among the merry makers, who were full of frolic and spritely capers . . . cut the 'pigeon's wing' and did the fancy steps. George McKensie bowed and smiled at his fair partner and Procter Humphrey swung 'em because he liked 'em. . . . The old ladies sat and looked on, nodding their approval, while the old gentlemen sat in the chimney corner and told stories of the days when they were young.[29]

Fourth of July 1853:

The day was very warm like all days in the Valley of late. The Social Hall was filled in the evening, and hundreds retired for the want of seats. The school houses in the 14th Ward were filled with prayers, and music and dancing and speeches, and picnics, and joy, and gladness.[30]

What They Danced

The earliest Mormon settlers in the Salt Lake Valley brought with them an Eastern Seaboard culture, including New England contra dances, quadrilles, and cotillions. According to Dorothy Shaw, "No group did a better job of carrying the best of American [dancing] culture across the continent than the Mormons, and they hung onto it long and well."[31]

In addition to the dances presented in this collection, the pioneers even danced the courtly minuet. Maypole dances were popular, featuring the "Queen of the May," and morris dancing was also mentioned. The Scandinavians brought their national folk dances and danced around the Christmas tree singing carols. Solo dances, such as the Highland fling and step dancing, were performed during dance party intermissions. Spanish Fork, Utah, was first settled by converts from Wales. One of the converts, Thomas Jenkins, was an exceptionally fine step dancer who "danced all the national jigs, step dancing and clogs of Wales, England, Ireland, and Scotland."[32]

Brigham Young himself was described as "acquitting himself very well on the light fantastic toe."[33] He loved dances with intricate footwork, ones that brought "sweat to the brow, and vigor to the body."

How They Danced

Entrance fees to the dances consisted of candles to light the hall, wood to stoke the fireplace, molasses, flour, corn, beans, cotton, pumpkin, squash, potatoes, eggs, carrots, butter, meat, animal fur, and even a live chicken or pig. These items were divided up to pay the band musicians.

The dances were family affairs. Mothers put their babies to sleep in baskets, boxes, or bundles of blankets. During the early part of the evening, the older children would join some of the dancing and the younger ones would romp through the dancers. As the night wore on, the children would tire and sleep on the benches. This delightful mingling of parents, children, and friends served to "stabilize the moral phase of pioneer life."[34]

Dance parties were always opened and closed with prayer. Intermission included songs and musical numbers, dramatic readings, speeches, and toasts, along with the specialty dance numbers. Refreshments of pies, cakes, and doughnuts were served, and sometimes a whole meal if the dance lasted into the wee hours of morning, though these hours were frowned upon by some as excessive.

Spirit and Style of the Dancing

Perhaps the best description of the spirit and style of Mormon pioneer dancing was written by Colonel Kane: "None of your minuets or other mortuary processions of gentiles in etiquette, tight shoe and pinching glove, but the spirited and scientific displays of our venerated and merry grandparents, who were not above following the fiddle to the lively fox-chase, French fours, Copenhagen jigs, Virginia reels, and the like forgotten figures executed with the spirit of a people too happy to be slow, or bashful or restrained."[35]

Brigham Young was known to say, "We'll show those gentiles how we dance before the Lord!" This was a natural feeling of proud defiance. The act of dancing as they crossed the plains was a way of "thumbing their noses" at the mobbers and persecutors. It was a way of saying, "You haven't crushed our spirits!"

Etiquette and Manners

Dancing schools were established in Salt Lake City and in many other communities. Masters of the art of dancing taught the children, as well as the older folks, the intricate figures and steps, "The acquisition of which gave them an ease and dignity of bearing."[36] The dancers paid exact attention to the proper steps of each dance, since it was considered "a violation of etiquette to do otherwise." Floor managers and callers kept strict order. These dancing schools provided social development and wholesome recreation. Most dancing manuals of this era, utilized by the dancing masters, contained voluminous chapters on all the fine points of etiquette for the dance.

Rules

From 1870 to 1871 in Randolf, Utah, the Church-sponsored dances were very strictly run by a committee appointed by the bishop. The following set of rules were created by the stake and sent to be enforced by the bishop of each ward:

1. Dances shall be conducted under the direction of the bishop, who will be held responsible for the manner in which they are conducted.
2. Dances shall be opened and closed with prayer and not be held after 12 p.m.
3. Waltzes or other round dances will not be countenanced in our assemblies.
4. Persons dancing out of their turn shall be considered violators of good order, and may be requested to retire [and may be rejected].
5. We will not use liquor in our assemblies, nor suffer any person intoxicated.
6. Swinging with an arm around the lady's waist shall not be permitted.
7. To swing a lady more than once against her will shall be considered ungentlemanly. To swing more than twice under any conditions shall be disorderly and [the young man will be] requested to retire.
8. Club dances gotten up to make money will not be countenanced unless specially ordered by the stake president or bishop.[37]

Why They Danced

To summarize, the Mormon pioneers danced to show thanksgiving and praise to God, to celebrate. They danced to raise their spirits and combat the losses and hardships of the pioneer experience. They danced to mentally and physically rejuvenate. They danced to make their bodies vigorous and strong. They danced to develop social grace, ease, and dignity of bearing. They danced to build morale and good fellowship. They danced to learn to move and work together. They danced to bond and create community. They danced to meet their mate. They danced to keep warm, relieve stress, play, and assimilate diverse cultures. Most of all, they danced to become one as a people, to build up the kingdom of God, and to establish their new Zion in the West.

Notes

1. Leona Holbrook, "Dancing as an Aspect of Early Mormon and Utah Culture," *Brigham Young University Studies* vol. 16, no. 1 (1975): 123.

2. Cecil E. McGavin, *The Mormon Pioneers* (Salt Lake City: Stevens and Wells, Inc., 1947): 159–60.

3. Holbrook, "Dancing as an Aspect of Early Mormon and Utah Culture," 122.

4. Thomas F. O'Dea, *The Mormons* (Chicago: University of Chicago, 1957): 129, quoting The Book of Mormon, 2 Nephi 2:25.

5. Ronald W. Walker and D. Michael Quinn, "'Virtuous, Lovely or of Good Report': How the Church Fostered the Arts," *Ensign*, July 1977, 83.

6. Holbrook, "Dancing as an Aspect of Early Mormon and Utah Culture," 121.

7. Brigham Young, *Discourses of Brigham Young*, comp. John A. Widtsoe (Salt Lake City: Deseret Book, 1954), 368, 375.

8. Davis Bitton, "These Licentious Days, Dancing Among the Mormons," *Sunstone Magazine*, May 1976, 18.

9. William Clayton, *An Intimate Chronicle, The Journals of William Clayton*, edited by George D. Smith (Salt Lake City: Signature Books 1955): 224.

10. Brigham Young, quoted in McGavin, *The Mormon Pioneers*, 31.

11. Marguerite Cameron, *This is the Place* (Caldwell: Caxton Press, 1939), 98.

12. Brigham Young, quoted in Leona Holbrook, "Dancing as an Aspect of Early Mormon and Utah Culture," *Brigham Young University Studies* vol 16, no. 1 (1975): 125.

13. Milton R. Hunter, *Utah in Her Western Setting* (Salt Lake City). The Mormons were not the only pioneers to dance at night while crossing the plains. Dancing was enjoyed by Mormons and non-Mormon pioneers alike in the nineteenth-century westward movement.

14. Clayton S. Rice, *The Mormon Way* (Salt Lake City: self-published, 1929), 61–62.

15. Carol Crofts Barney, great-granddaughter of John and Ellen Crofts, interview by author, June 2016.

16. Thomas L. Kane, *The Mormons* (Philadelphia: King and Band, 1840), 29–32.

17. Kate B. Carter, "Dancing—A Pioneer Recreation," *Treasures of Pioneer History* vol. 1 (Salt Lake City: Daughters of Utah Pioneers, 1952), 361.

18. John Hyde, quoted in Andrew Love Neff, *History of Utah 1847 to 1869* (Salt Lake City: Deseret News Press, 1940), 599.

19. Richard Burton, quoted in Neff, *History of Utah 1847 to 1869*, 599–600.

20. Wallace Stegner, *Mormon Country* (New York: Bonanza Books, 1942), 64.

21. Young, *Discourses of Brigham Young*, 373.

22. Stegner, *Mormon Country*, 25.

23. Holbrook, "Dancing as an Aspect of Early Mormon and Utah Culture," 138.

24. Lois S. Brown, "Waltz to the Rescue," *Saga of the Sanpitch* vol. 18 (Mt. Pleasant, Utah: North Sanpete Publishing, 1986), 4–5.

25. George Templeton Strong, quoted in Cyrus R. K. Patell and Bryan Waterman, *The Cambridge Companion to the Literature of New York* (New York: Cambridge University Press, 2010), 19.

26. Donna M. Hogge (master's thesis, 1948), 27.

27. Levi Edgar Young, *The Founding of Utah* (New York: Charles Scribner's Sons, 1923), 332.

28. Susan A. Madsen, *Christmas, A Joyful Heritage* (Salt Lake City: Deseret Book 1984), 33.

29. Don Carlos Johnson, *A Brief History of Springville, Utah* (Springville, Utah: William F. Gibson, 1900), 17–18.

30. Young, *The Founding of Utah*, 333–34.

31. Dorothy Shaw, *The Story of Square Dancing, A Family Tree* (Los Angeles: Sets In Order, 1967), 14.

32. Carter, "Dancing—A Pioneer Recreation," 396.

33. Rex Austin Skidmore, "Mormon Recreation in Theory and Practice: A Study of Social Change" (PhD diss., University of Pennsylvania, 1941), 40.

34. Lydia Walker Forsgren, *History of Box Elder County* (Salt Lake City: Daughters of Utah Pioneers, 1937), 170.

35. Thomas L. Kane, quoted in Edward W. Tullidge, *History of Salt Lake City* (Salt Lake City: Star Printing Company, 1886), 31–32.

36. Carter, *Treasures of Pioneer History*, 361–62.

37. Della Mckinnan, "History of Randolph Utah," (Salt Lake City: Daughters of Utah Pioneers Museum Archives, unpublished).

Part Two

TEN DANCES FOR TREK REENACTMENTS, FAMILY REUNIONS, AND COMMUNITY CELEBRATIONS

The Grand March

"The Grand March" was the official opener for nineteenth-century balls. It is a ceremonial processional where all the participants were "on display to be viewed in a dignified fashion."[1] Brigham Young maintained it was not a proper ball unless it commenced with "The Grand March." This is an arrangement of some typical Grand March figures.

FORMATION: The dance starts with the host or lead couple taking several turns around the room gathering up couples who follow the lead couple, couple behind couple, until all are gathered. It is helpful for the first few couples to be familiar with the dance so the others can follow.

STEP: Walking.

MUSIC: "Bonaparte Crossing the Rhine," "Jimmy Allen," and "Marching Through Georgia."

Figure 1

DIVIDE AND SINGLE FILE. Host couple leads the couples up the center of the room toward the band. Partners cast off, gents go left and ladies right, single file. Circling around the room in opposite directions, they meet and pass, first with the gents on the outside of the circle. When they meet again at the top of the room, the ladies pass on the outside of the circle.

Figure 2

DANISH MARCH. Partners meet at the bottom and come up the center to form a longways set with partners facing. The top, or lead, couple joins two hands, while the lines move apart to accommodate them as they sashay down the center. The rest of the couples follow the two hand Chassez with the two lines moving up on the side. Couples are separating at the bottom to join onto the lines until the lead couple is once again at the top.

Figure 3

MARCH OF THE PLATOONS. All couples join inside hands to face up the set. Couples cast off with the first couple left, second right, and so on around the room again.

Figure 4

ARCHES AND/OR ARCH AND DIVE. When the couple lines meet at the bottom, the lead couple's line lifts inside hands to arch over other line. When they meet at the top, the other line arches. (An alternate version is to arch and dive with first couple arching, then diving under the next couple's arch, continuing to arch and dive through the two lines of couples, and repeating this when they meet again at the top of the room.)

Figure 5

FOUR ABREAST/SNAIL. Couples meet at the bottom of the room to come up 4 abreast. First line of 4 pulls around with the second line of 4 latching on, forming a line that serpentines through the four couple lines of 4, adding the next line of 4 as they pass. This line pulls around into a circle. It then wraps into a snail and out to a final circle. All balance four steps into the center and back twice, to end with a partner salute.

Sources

Carol Teten, "A Nineteenth Century Ballroom: The Charm of Group Dances," *How to Dance Through Time* vol. VI, (2001; Kentfield, 2003), DVD; Patri J. Pulglise, *Dances for The Civil War Ballroom* (Lanesboro: Stellar Production, 2011), 23–29.

Bonapart Crossing the Rhine

Irish Traditional

Jimmy Allen

New England Traditional

Marching through Georgia

The Virginia Reel

The Virginia reel was the most popular dance of the Mormon pioneers crossing the plains. Often, after traveling fifteen miles mostly on foot, they would set up camp, have dinner, and sing some hymns. Then the fiddler would play and the pioneers would dance. A verse from the Mormon folk song about the trek, "Wo Haw Buck and Jerry Boys," sung to the tune of "Turkey in the Straw," describes this as follows:

> Oh, tonight we'll dance by the light of the moon,
> To the fiddler's best and only tune.
> Holdin' her hand and stealin' a kiss,
> Never a step of the dance we miss.
> Never did know a love like this!
> Wo Haw Buck and Jerry Boys!

The Dance

FORMATION: Longways sets of five to six couples facing opposite each other. Gents are on one side, with L. shoulder to the music, and ladies on the other side.

STEPS: Brisk walking and Chassez.

MUSIC: "Western Country," "Soldier's Joy," "Angeline the Baker," "Mississippi Sawyer," "Yellow Rose of Texas." It is best to have a medley of tunes since the Virginia Reel often lasts a long time, due to folks joining on the end of the line when they see the dancers having so much fun.

A1 8 bars	BALANCE: Both lines balance walking forward 4 and back 4 twice to their partner acknowledging (or nodding at) them each time they meet (**16 total**).
A2 8 bars	RIGHT HANDS ROUND: Partners walk forward to turn R. hands once around and back to place (8).

LEFT HANDS ROUND: Partners walk forward to turn L. hands around and back to place (8) (**16 total**).

B1 8 bars TWO HANDS ROUND: Partners walk forward to take a two-hand CW turn and back to place (8).

DOS-A-DOS: Partners walk forward to pass R. shoulders, slide to the right back to back, then back up, passing L. shoulders, to place (8) (**16 total**).

B2 8 bars TOP COUPLE CHASSEZ TO THE BOTTOM AND BACK: The top couple takes two hands and Chassez (8) to the bottom of the set, and (8) back to the top (**16 total**).

THE REEL OR "STRIP THE WILLOW": Top couple hooks R. elbows to turn once and a half to face the opposite gender line, then hooks L. elbows once around with that next couple, then turns their partner once with the R. elbow, then left with the next couple down the set, repeating this with all subsequent couples down to the bottom of the set.

(This can take any number of counts, depending on the dancers' experience. It's most satisfying where it can be kept to the phrase of the music.)

CHASSEZ TO THE TOP: The active couple sashays to the top, making sure they are on their proper side of the set.

(This is a good time to bring all the sets back together by signaling the faster sets to wait so all sets can Walk the Highway together.)

WALK THE HIGHWAY: The top couple casts off, or separates, to go down the outside of the set with the two lines following. (When teaching, I use the metaphor "peel the banana.") Top couple makes a TWO-HAND BRIDGE at the bottom of the set for each couple to take inside hands and walk under, up the set leaving the top couple at the bottom.

The dance starts over again with a new top couple.

(Here again, the amount of counts is variable, but it is most satisfying to restart the dance with Forward and Back on the phrase of the music.)

NOTE: The Virginia Reel descends from several, more formal, eighteenth-century British dances, including Sir Roger de Coverley.

(With brand new dancers and smaller children, it is often preferable to leave out the Reel or "Strip the Willow" figure.)

Soldier's Joy

American Traditional

Angeline the Baker

American Traditional

Mississippi Sawyer

American Traditional

The Yellow Rose of Texas

American Traditional

Haste to the Wedding

This dance crossed the Atlantic in the 1850s and showed up in the Mormon pioneer repertoire. It originates from Sussex and Dorset, England.[2] The pioneers from England brought it to Zion, where it is still danced today in living tradition.

The Dance

FORMATION: Longways proper sets of five or six couples facing, gents on one side and ladies on the other. Top couple only is active, though it also can be danced with every other couple active as in a contra dance.

STEPS: Walking.

MUSIC: "Haste to the Wedding" is the tune traditionally used in Utah and England. It is also danced to the tune, "Pop! Goes the Weasel."

A1 8 bars	LADY DOWN THE CENTER AND GENT OUTSIDE: Top couple walks to the bottom of the set, lady down the center, and gent down the outside (8), and return (8) (**16 total**).
A2 8 bars	GENT DOWN THE CENTER AND LADY OUTSIDE: Top couple walks again to the bottom of the set, gent down the center, and lady down the outside (8) and return (8) (**16 total**).
B1 6 bars	TOPS CIRCLE SECOND LADY: Top couple circles left with the second lady (12).
2 bars	POP TO THE TOP: On count 13, or the word "pop," they raise their joined hands to "pop" the second lady through this arch to top place (4). (This requires a bit of calculation so the lady ends at the top of the set—a quick twice around or a leisurely once around.) (**16 total**)
B2 8 bars	Repeat B1 with the second gent.

The dance starts over again with the second couple now in top place while the former top couple Chassez down the center to the bottom of the set and the rest of the couples move up the set one place.

SOURCES: Craig R. Miller, *An Old-Time Utah Dance Party* (Salt Lake City: Utah Arts Council, 2000), 59; Rickey Holden, *The Contra Dance Book* (Newark: American Squares, 1956), 90.

Haste to the Wedding

New England Traditional

Pop Goes the Weasel

Oslo Waltz

This dance is a popular waltz circle mixers. Its country of origin would appear to be Norway, with figures resembling the Scandinavian "Familie Vals." However, many sources claim it to be of British origin. Along with other religious leaders of his day, Brigham Young frowned on the waltz but tolerated it in a structured formation without partners in closed ballroom position. However, a suppression of the waltz proved difficult since so many Scandinavian converts immigrated to Utah, bringing with them their national folk dances, including the couple turning waltz.

The Dance:

FORMATION: Couples in a single circle with everyone holding hands, lady on the gent's right.

STEPS: Waltz balance, back-to-back/face-to-face, two-hand or couple waltz turn.

MUSIC: "The Black Hills Waltz." (This tune was composed along the pioneer trail to Utah.)

Figure 1

A1 and A2 — BALANCE/LEAD LADY ACROSS: Couples balance in and out of the circle (forward touch, back touch) while swinging arms forward and back (2). Gent leads the lady on his left across to his right (partner's position) in 2 waltz steps. This is repeated 3 more times, 4 times in all (**16 total**).

Figure 2

B1 — BACK-TO-BACK AND FACE-TO-FACE: With this new partner, couples face line of dance with inside hands joined, and dance forward CCW one waltz step back-to-back, pushing joined hands forward, then one waltz step face-to-face, swinging hands backwards (2).

Repeat back-to-back/face-to-face, 4 waltz steps in all, turning halfway around a fourth time to face CW. Repeat back-to-back and face-to-face as above in this direction to end with partners facing (**8 total**).

Figure 3

B2 TWO-HAND WALTZ TURN: Couples dance a Two-Hand Turn in place with 8 waltz steps, opening out into a single circle on measures 7 and 8 with the lady on the right of the gent to start the dance over again (**8 total**).

B2 Alternate COUPLE-TURNING WALTZ: In place of the two-hand waltz turn, couples may take ballroom position and dance four waltz turns in 8 waltz steps progressing CCW in line of dance.

Source

Craig R. Miller, *An Old-Time Utah Dance Party* (Salt Lake City: Utah Arts Council, 2000), 64.

Black Hills Waltz

(section ABB)

American Traditional

Spanish Waltz

(Over the Waves)

The Spanish waltz is a nineteenth-century, couple-facing-couple dance, done in either a longways set or Sicilian circle formation. This dance was enjoyed at the height of its popularity during the American Civil War and has been handed down through generations from the Mormon pioneer era to the present

The Dance

FORMATION: Two couples facing each other in a longways set or CW and CCW in a Sicilian circle. The longways set progression is like a contra dance, with first couples moving down the set and seconds moving up the set.

STEP: Waltz

MUSIC: Spanish Waltz

A1 4 bars	BALANCE/TURN QUARTER: Couples join inside hands and balance forward and back. Using inside hands (gent's right/lady's left), gent turns opposite lady under his R. arm a quarter. All couples end up facing their partner across the set of 4 with a waltz balance step back (**4 total**).
4 bars	REPEAT ABOVE FIGURE. Couples end up facing up or down the set, with their partner by their side but opposite from original position (**4 total**).
A2 8 bars	REPEAT ALL OF FIGURE A1. End in original position (**8 total**).
B1 8 bars	HANDS ACROSS: The two couples R. hand star with 4 waltz steps, and L. hand star with 4 waltz steps back to place (**8 total**).
B2 8 bars	PROMENADE AROUND: Couples dance a pinwheel, in promenade position, with gents' L. shoulders together rotating once and halfway

around to progress on to the next couple (**8 total**).

B2 Variation 1 BALANCE AND COUPLES WALTZ PAST: Couples waltz balance forward two waltz steps and back two, then waltz pass on the right as a couple progressing on to the next couple.

B2 Variation 2 1 1/2 COUPLE TURNING WALTZ AROUND: Couples assume ballroom position and waltz turn around each other, as in a 1 1/2 Dos-a-Dos to progress on to the next couple.

Suggested movements for top and bottom couples left out of the longways set.

A1 and A2 TWO-HAND BALANCE FORWARD AND BACK: Gent turns Lady under R. hand, repeated four times.

B1 COUPLES R. HAND SINGLE STAR ONCE AROUND: Return with L. hand.

B2 TWO-HAND CIRCLE LEFT: Opening up to face up, or down, the set, on last four bars with the lady on the right.

SOURCES: Craig R. Miller, *An Old-Time Utah Dance Party* (Salt Lake City: Utah Arts Council, 2000), 64; Patri J. Pulglise, *Dances for The Civil War Ballroom* (Lanesboro: Stellar Production, 2011), 76; Henry Tolman, *The Welcome Guest* (New York: S. T. Gordon, 1863), 200.

Spanish Waltz

American Traditional

Danish Slide-Off

Danish converts were the second largest immigrant group to come to Utah. Between 1850 and 1875, more than thirty thousand Danish converts crossed the ocean and the plains to settle there, bringing their dances, music, and culture with them. The tune for this dance is found in *Pioneer Songs*, published by the Daughters of Utah Pioneers. There are several different dances done to this tune. This particular version has survived since pioneer times in living tradition in St. George, Utah.

The Dance

FORMATION: Couples facing in two-hand position in a double circle with the gent's back to the center. The couples may also dance it randomly scattered around the room, still moving in a CCW direction.

STEPS: Side-close, slide (Chassez), and step-hop

MUSIC: "Danish Slide Off"[3]

A1 4 bars	SIDE-CLOSE/DOUBLE TIME SLIDE: Starting LOD with gent's L. foot and lady's right, side-close four times. Seven double-time slides in the same direction ending with a step-close (**16 total**).
A2 4 bars	Repeat above in opposite direction, RLOD (**16 total**).
B1 4 bars	STEP-HOP/RIGHT ELBOW HOOK TURN: Couple hooks R. elbows, turning twice in place with eight step-hops (**16 total**).
B2 4 bars	STEP-HOP LOD/LEFT ELBOW HOOK: Couple hooks L. elbows, and the gent backs up with eight step-hops while the lady takes eight step-hops forward LOD. Elbows staying linked (**16 total**).

MIXER: This dance can be made into a mixer in B2 by having the lady moving forward to the new partner in 4 step-hops while the gent takes those 4 step-hops in place. They link L. elbows on the last four step-hops to continue moving in LOD.

VARIATION: I learned the following version to the same music from a Danish woman at the Seattle 2009 Pourparler Conference.

A1 and A2 COUPLE POLKA: Couples in ballroom position take eight CW polka turns in LOD around a circle, ending with their joined hands pointing into the center of the circle (**16 total**).

B1 SIDE-CLOSE/SLIDE: Take four slow step-closes into the center with opposite feet (gent's left, lady's right) Step-close, step-close, step-close, step (hold), followed by eight double-time slides in opposite directions, away from the center of the circle (8).

B2 Repeat B1 (**16 total**).

SOURCE: Craig R. Miller, *An Old-Time Utah Dance Party* (Salt Lake City: Utah Arts Council, 2000), 56.

Danish Slide Off

Danish Traditional

Oak City Quadrille

The following quadrille has been danced in Oak City, Utah, since the founding of the town by the Mormon pioneers in 1865. It is currently danced at town celebrations such as weddings and Oak City Days. The word "quadrille" is pronounced "ka-drill" by locals in rural Utah communities where the quadrille has been preserved. As in nineteenth-century quadrille tradition, the Oak City Quadrille is memorized and succinctly prompted by the caller, with very little "patter."

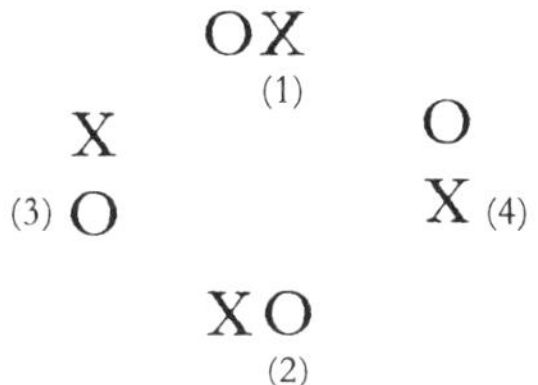

The Dance

FORMATION: Four couples in a quadrille, or square formation.

MUSIC: Each figure is accompanied by a completely different tune.

STEP: Brisk walking, balance

Figure 1: Circle Three and Switch (32 bars)

16-COUNT INTRO

TUNE: "The Girl I Left Behind Me"

A1 8 bars	AROUND THE OUTSIDE: Couple #1 turns back-to-back and separates to walk around the outside of the square, passing each other by the R. shoulder, continuing around the outside of the circle to their home position (**16 total**).
A2 8 bars	CIRCLE THREE: Couple #1 passes each other again by L. shoulders to circle 3 left twice with

	the sides, lady with couple #3 and gent with couple #4 (**16 total**).
B1 8 bars	SWITCH: Lady and gent of #1 switches places, with #1 gent circling left and right with couple #3 and lady #1 circling with couple #4 (**16 total**).
B2 8 bars	ALL BALANCE PARTNER AND SWING: All return to home position to balance (forward touch, back touch) and Two-Hand Swing partner 15–16 (**16 total**).

Repeat this figure three more times with couples 2, 3, and 4.

Figure 2: Alamo Style

TUNE: "Johnny Blevin's Quadrille"

16-COUNT INTRO B2

A1	CIRCLE LEFT ONCE AROUND. All join hands and circle left once around (**16 total**).
A2	LADIES BALANCE/GENTS BALANCE: Ladies walk 4 to the center and back 4. Gents do the same (**16 total**).
B1	HEADS BALANCE: Head couples walk forward 4 and back 4 (8). Sides Balance: Side couples do the same (8) (**16 total**).
B2	All join hands into the center 4 and back 4 (8). All Two-Hand Swing partner (8) (**16 total**).
A1 4 bars	ALAMO STYLE FIGURE: Partners face, take R. hands, and pull each other across, as in a Grand Right and Left, to take the next person's L. hand, keeping hold of partner's R. hand. This forms a wavy circle (ladies facing in and gents facing out of the circle). Balance forward touch, back touch (8).

4 bars	REPEAT: Drop partner's R. hand to pull-by with joined L. hands to turn halfway around, joining R. hands with next person in the wavy circle (ladies now face out, gents face in). Repeat balance (8) (**16 total**).

(This figure is a Grand Right and Left with balances all the way around the ring.)

A2, B1, B2	REPEAT ALAMO STYLE FIGURE: Making a total of seven half turns, balance forward and back. Meet partner (for a second time) and quickly R. hand turn partner once around, opening out in home position (**48 total**). Repeat all of the above.

Figure 3: Grand Cut-a-Sha[4]

TUNE: "John Perry's Quadrille"

16-COUNT INTRO

A1 8 bars	CIRCLE LEFT AND RIGHT: All join hands in one big ring to circle left (8) and back to the right (**16 total**).
A2 8 bars	HEADS AND SIDES BALANCE: Head couples forward 4 and back 4. Side Couples forward 4 and back 4 (**16 total**).
B1 8 bars	HEADS CUT-A SHA ("cutta shaw"): Head couples walk forward and take R. hands with the opposite, then turn only a quarter to take L. hands with partner, then turn a quarter to take R. hands with opposite then turn a quarter to meet partner with L. hands Dancers are taking alternate hands around a square, gents keep turning left, ladies turning right a quarter (**16 total**).

(This figure is the same as Square Through in Western Square dance and Rights and Lefts in English country dance, a Mini Right and Left Grand.)

B2 8 bars — DOS-A-DOS CORNER/TWO-HAND SWING PARTNERS: On the end of the above figure, couples one and two pull partners by with L. hands to Dos-a-Dos corners (8). All Two-Hand Swing partners once around CW (8) (**16 total**).

Repeat this figure three more times with sides, then heads, then sides again, four times in all.

Figure 4: Moulinet Mixer

TUNE: "Golden Slippers" 16 count intro.

A1 8 bars — CIRCLE LEFT AND RIGHT: All join hands and circle left (8) and back to the right (8) (**16 total**).

A1 8 bars — LADIES BALANCE/GENTS BALANCE: Ladies walk 4 to the center and 4 back. Gents do the same (**16 total**).

B1 8 bars — LADIES HANDS ACROSS: Ladies take R. hands across to star for 8, then star back with the left 8, passing their partner by (**16 total**).

B2 4 bars — MOULINET: The lady takes the next gent with hand hold (lady's R. and gent's L. hands), forming a large moulinet (Texas Star), which progresses CCW back to the woman's original home position (**16 total**).

4 bars — Everyone balance and Two-Hand Swing this new partner (**16 total**).

Repeat figure 3 until everyone has returned to their original partner and home position.

When I filmed this quadrille at the Oak City Days festival in 1998, the following tunes were played: "Oh Susanna," "Golden

Slippers," "Camp Town Racetrack," "Jingle Bells," "The Saints Go Marching In," "The Bear Went over the Mountain," "Yankee Doodle," and "She'll Be Comin' Round the Mountain." The quadrille was danced "unphrased"—no fitting of the figures to the music phrase. For the purpose of ease in teaching and learning this quadrille, I have arranged the figures to fit the music phrase emulating a nineteenth-century-era quadrille.

Nineteenth-century quadrilles were performed "with pageantry," with walking, or "gliding in a wavy and graceful manner," especially when danced at a formal ball.[5] Today, during Oak City Days, the teens have taken over dancing this quadrille with great enthusiasm, whoops, hollers, and knee slapping. They *love* this quadrille, and beg the caller to prompt it. I have also observed this quadrille danced by adults in a more organized and stately fashion at a wedding in Oak City.

The Girl I Left Behind Me

Irish Traditional

Johnny Blevin's Quadrille

American Traditional

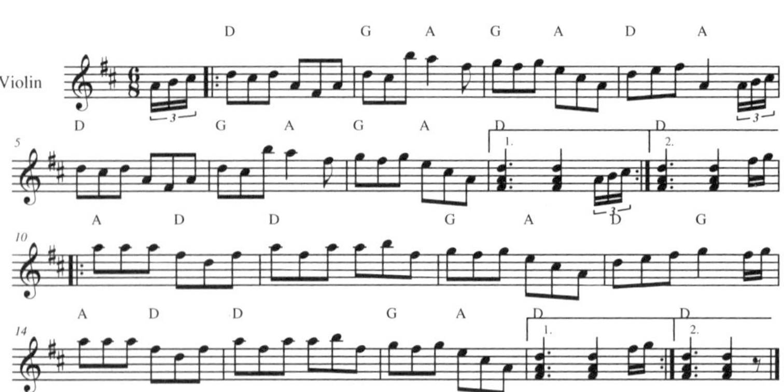

John Perry's Quadrille

American Traditional

Golden Slippers

American Traditional

Heel-Toe Polka

Nineteenth-century dancing masters denounced the polka, "this rowdy, raucous dance form," as a "deterioration in the general tone of motion and manner."[6] However, Brigham Young favored the polka because it was vigorous and energetic.

The Dance

FORMATION: Partners begin in closed ballroom, or two-hand position, and progress CCW around the room, scattered or in a circle.

STEPS: Heel-toe, slide, (Chassez), couple turning polka

MUSIC: "Jenny Lind Polka"

A1 HEEL-TOE/SLIDE: Partners are facing with the gent's back to the center of the room. With gent's L. and lady's R. foot, they take 2 heel-toe steps and 4 slides LOD (4). They repeat this with opposite feet RLOD (**8 total**).

A2 COUPLE POLKA TURN: In ballroom position, couple dances 8 polka CW turning steps in LOD around the room (**8 total**).

B1 and B2 repeat above sequence.

Variation 1: Heel-toe once and slide twice, repeat in opposite direction then take 4 polka steps, turning twice. Repeat.

Variation 2: Moving CCW, couples in ballroom position dance heel-toe, polka step, (half CW turn). Heel-toe, polka step (half CW turn) then take 4 polka steps, turning twice.

TEACHING STRATEGY FOR COUPLE TURNING POLKA

1. Dancers in a single circle take 8 slides to their right LOD.
2. Hopping on R. foot to turn halfway to the right (CW) to face out and take 8 slides to their left LOD.

3. Hopping on L. foot to turn halfway to the right (CW) to face in and take 8 slides to their right LOD.
4. Reduce slides first to 4, then 2, then 1, which has now magically become a CW polka turning step.
5. Put couples together to practice the couple-turning polka.

SOURCES: Craig R. Miller, *An Old-Time Utah Dance Party* (Salt Lake City: Utah Arts Council, 2000), 59; Lucille K. Czarnowski, *Dances of Early California Days* (Palo Alto: Pacific Books, 1950), 123; Lloyd Shaw, *The Round Dance Book: A Century of Waltzing* (Caldwell: Caxton Printers, 1948), 74.

Jenny Lind Polka

American Traditional

Violin

The Patty Cake Polka

This dance is a variation on the Heel-Toe Polka, which is quickly taught and instantly enjoyed. It is a section from the longer, Victorian dance, "The Jenny Lind." It is often danced to the tune "Jenny Lind Polka," composed to honor Jenny Lind, a world-famous singer of that era known as the "Swedish Nightingale." Many variations of this popular dance are found all over Europe and America.

The Dance

FORMATION: Couples are facing in a single circle with a two-hand hold, ladies facing CW and gents CCW. This dance can also be done with couples scattered about the room.

STEPS: Heel-toe, Chassez (slide) and walk or skip.

MUSIC: "The Cuckoo Polka." Alternate tunes: "Jenny Lind Polka" and "Buffalo Gals"[7]

A1 HEEL-TOE/CHASSEZ: Starting gent's left and lady's right, heel-toe, heel-toe, 4 slides into the circle closing on 4 with (weight on gent's left and lady's right).

Repeat with opposite footwork moving out of the circle (**16 total**).

A2 Repeat A1 above Heel-Toe/Chassez (**16 total**).

B1 PATTY CAKE: Clap R. hands with partner 3 times. Clap L. hands 3 times. Clap both hands 3 times and on own knees 3 times (8).

ELBOW TURN: Hook R. elbows and walk or skip once or twice around for 8 counts (**16 total**).

B2 Repeat B1 Patty Cake and Elbow Turn.

MIXER: Move forward to a new partner (Ladies CW, Gents CCW) on the end of B2 to start the dance over again.

SOURCE: Interview with Pattie Richards, a traditional musician who grew up playing with her parents for the old-time dances throughout Utah's Uinta Basin.

The Cuckoo Polka

American Traditional

Jenny Lind Polka

American Traditional

Notes for Ten Dances

1. Carol Teten, "A Nineteenth Century Ballroom: The Charm of Group Dances," *How to Dance through Time* vol. 6, (2001; Kentfield, 2003), DVD.

2. Douglas Kennedy, *Community Dance Manual* (London: English Folk Dance and Song Society, 1967), 114.

3. This tune is included in the *Daughters of Utah Pioneers' Pioneer Songs*, 274. In Denmark, Fastelavn is a holiday just before Lent, which is celebrated much like Halloween, where children dress up in costumes and go door-to-door begging for treats while singing a song to this Danish Slide-Off tune.

Lyrics from This Fastelavn song roughly translated here into English.

Fastelavn is my name
I want to have candy
If I don't get any candy
Then I will make mischief
Candy up,
Candy down,
Candy in my tummy
If I don't get any candy
Then I will make mischief

4. The "Cut-a-Sha" appears to be a local term for this figure since it also appears in quadrille dance notes for "Irish Washerwoman" on page 273 of *Pioneer Songs*, Daughters of Utah Pioneer's publication.

5. Teten, "A Nineteenth Century Ballroom."

6. Paul Magriel, *Chronicles of the American Dance* (New York: Exposition Press, 1957), 90.

7. The sheet music for this dance is not included in this book. See The Lester S. Levy Sheet Music Collection,

"Campbell's Melodies: Buffalo Gals," *Johns Hopkins University*, levysheetmusic.mse.jhu.edu/catalog/levy:018.037.

FIVE CHILDREN'S SONG DANCES

Oh! Susanna!

This is another song-dance enjoyed by children and adults alike. Stephen Foster composed this song in 1846, and it has become one of the most popular American songs.

The Dance

FORMATION: This dance starts with partners holding hands in a single circle facing center. The gent is on the left and the lady on the right. With parent/child couples, have the parent on the left and child on the right.

STEP: Walking

MUSIC: "Oh! Susanna!"

SONG	MOVEMENT
Oh, I come from Alabama with my banjo on my knee.	All walk 4 steps into the center of the circle, and 4 steps back.
I'm going to Louisiana for my true love for to see.	Repeat (**16 total**)
It rained all night the day I left, the weather it was dry. The sun so hot, I froze to death, Susanna don't you cry.	Partners face to take R. hands to do a R. and L. grand chain around the ring to about the 4th or 5th person. Ladies in CW direction, gents CCW (**16 total**).[1]

CHORUS

Oh! Susanna, oh don't you cry for me.
I come from Alabama with my banjo on my knee.

Couples take promenade position facing CCW, gent on left and lady on the right, to promenade around the circle, turning into a single circle on the end of the second time through the chorus to start the dance over (**16 total**).

Repeat chorus (**16 total**).

Oh! Susanna!
Stephen Foster
Oh, I come from Al - a - ba - ma with my ban - jo on my knee. I'm
going to Loui - si - an - a for my true love for to see. It
rained all night the day I left, the wea - ther it was dry. The
sun so hot, I froze to death, Su - san - na don't you cry.
Oh! Su - san - na, oh don't you cry for me. I
come from Al - a - ba - ma with my ban - jo on my knee.
Oh! Su - san - na, oh don't you cry for me. I
come from Al - a - ba - ma with my ban - jo on my knee.
Oh! Susanna!.lim

Somebody's Waiting

This is a traditional New England song-dance that has made its way out to Utah. It's a wonderful "win/win" children's dance game that also works well with families and mixed ages.

The Dance

FORMATION: Dancers are in a single circle, no partners, with one person in the center of the circle. In Part 2, the participants in the circle clap and sing while the choosing and swinging goes on in the middle. It is best to have more than one person in the center when there is a large crowd.

STEPS: Walking and skipping in the swing.

MUSIC: "There's Somebody's Waiting for Me"

SONG	MOVEMENTS
PART I	
When I looked into your eyes, I beheld a big surprise, There is somebody waiting for me.	Circle left, CW (**16 total**)
There is somebody waiting, there is somebody waiting, There is somebody waiting for me.	Circle right, CCW (**16 total**).
PART II	
Choose two leave the others, Choose two leave the others, Choose two and leave the others for me.	Middle person chooses two people from the circle. This threesome circles left in the center, while rest clap (**16 total**).
Swing one, leave the other, Swing one, leave the other, Swing one, leave the other, for me.	Middle person chooses one of the two to continue with a Two-Hand Swing (**16 total**).

(Part II, verse 1 can be sung twice if kids take longer to make a choice.)

The dance starts over again, the two swinging in the middle joining the circle. The leftover person becomes the new middle person who does the next choosing.

SOURCE: I first learned this song-dance from Marianne Taylor at Pourparler 2001 in Colrain, Massachusetts.

There's Somebody Waiting for Me

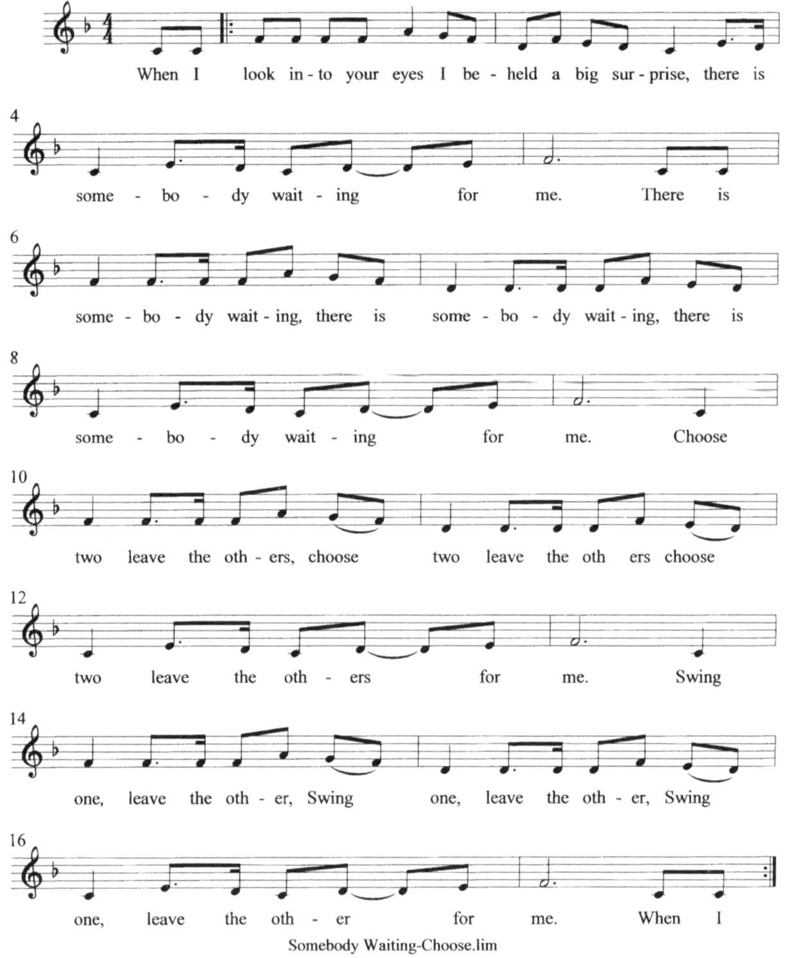

Pop Goes the Weasel

Children's Version

"Pop Goes the Weasel" was a popular tune during the 1850s and through the early 1900s in England and America. It was used in many dance forms, from longways sets, children's song-dances and games to a Morris stick dance. This particular children's song-dance is enjoyed by young and old alike. It is a wonderful family and community dance, with all ages dancing together.

The Dance

FORMATION: A circle made up with groups of threesomes, facing CCW like spokes on a wheel. The child in the middle of the threesome is the "popper," flanked on each side by the other two who have their inside hands joined behind the popper. and outside hands joined with those of the popper. When adults and children are dancing together it is best to put the smallest child in the middle as the popper.

STEP: Walk or skip

MUSIC: "Pop Goes the Weasel"

SONG	ACTION
All around the cobbler's bench, The monkey chased the weasel; The monkey thought 'twas all in fun,	All sing and walk or skip in LOD/CCW (**12 total**).
Pop! goes the weasel.	At the word *Pop!*, the "popper" drops both hands and hunkers down while the outside two arch over him to walk up to the next popper, who rises and without turning around and puts his hands out to be grasped by the outside two (**4 total**).

CHORUS

Penny for a spool of thread, Penny for a needle; That's the way the money goes, Pop! goes the weasel.[2]	Repeat the dance with this new trio (**16 total**).

Repeat the verse and song as many times as is fun for all. You may stop the dance after a few times and let another of the trio become the popper, or let the children switch positions on their own during the dance, once they know it well.

NOTE: Queen Victoria's dancing master, Joseph Lowe, reports teaching "Pop Goes the Weasel" to the royal children and their friends.[3]

MORE VERSES: The following two sets of verses may also be learned and utilized:

PART I

My mother taught me how to sew,
And how to thread the needle.
Every time my finger slips,
Pop! goes the weasel.
You may try to sew and sew,
And never make something regal.
So roll it up and let it go,
Pop! goes the weasel.

PART II

I went a 'hunting in the woods.
It wasn't very legal.
The dog and I were caught with the goods,
Pop! goes the weasel.
I said I didn't hunt or sport.
The warden looked at my beagle.
He said to tell it to the court,
Pop! goes the weasel.

SOURCE: Sanna Longden, *More Favorite Folk Dances* (1996; Evanston: FolkStyle Productions, 2004), DVD and Syllabus No. 2; used with permission.

Pop Goes the Weasel

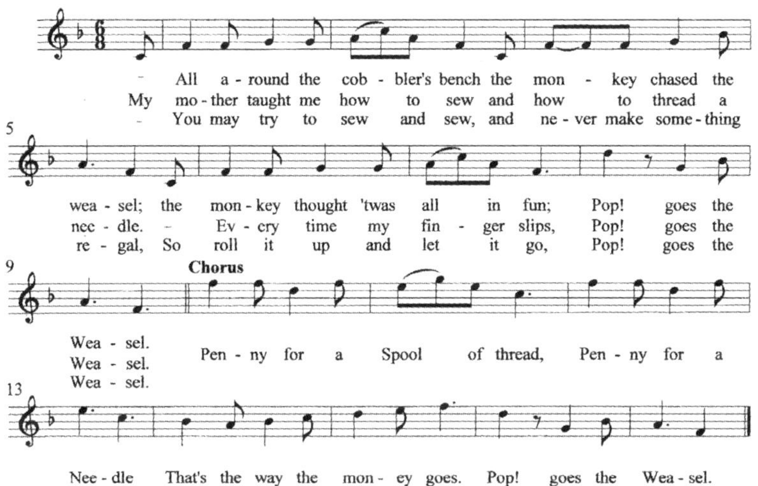

Gift to Be Simple

This is a popular children's song-dance set to this well-known Shaker song said to be a favorite of Brigham Young.[4] Shakers were contemporaries with the Mormons, and several Shakers converted to Mormonism. This dance was created by legendary New Hampshire caller, Dudley Laufman, and is performed in the quasi-Shaker style of acting out the movement words in the song.

The Dance

FORMATION: Longways proper set of five to six couples. This dance can be performed by children and adults. It works best at first when older children and adults are dancing with the younger ones, with the taller folks on the gents' side of the set.

STEPS: Walking

MUSIC: "Gift to Be Simple"

SONG	ACTION
'Tis a gift to be simple, tis a gift to be free. 'Tis a gift to come down where we ought to be.	Lines forward 4 and back 4 twice. Hands joined along the lines (**16 total**).
And when we find ourselves in a place just right,	All couples turn to join inside hands and walk down the set (8).
We will be in the valley of love and delight.	Couples turn and walk up the set (**16 total**).
When true simplicity is gained,	All two-hand arch (**8 total**).
To bow and to bend we shan't be ashamed	Top couple bends down to go through the arches to the bottom of the set (**16 total**).
To turn, turn will be our delight. Till by turning and turning, we turn 'round right.	Individual dancers turn in place once around CW to the right (8), then once CCW to the left (**16 total**).

This dance repeats with a new head couple each time until each couple has had a turn as head couple.

SOURCE: Dudley Laufman, *Traditional Barn Dances*, 100; used with permission.

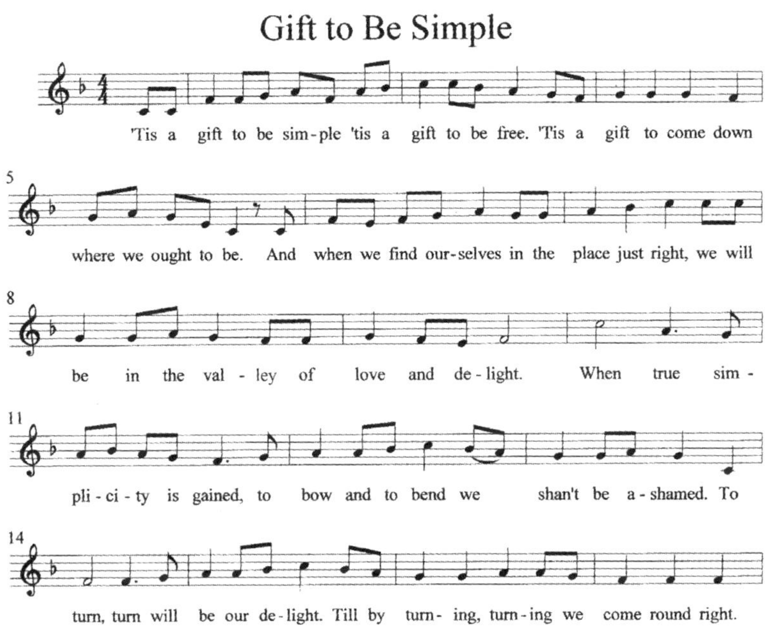

All Good Children

This is a children's version of the "Seven-Step Schottische" found in New England and Southern USA. According to Dudley Laufman, this "Seven Step Polka" comes from the Shetland Islands of Scotland and was even found on Native American reservations in North Dakota.

The Dance

FORMATION: Single circle, partners facing each other with two hands joined. Girls face CW, boys CCW. Small children do best with adults or older children for partners.

STEP: Walk, side-close, and step-hop.

MUSIC: "All Good Children"

SONG	FIGURE I
One, two, three, four, five, six, seven	Side-close, side-close, side-close, side-touch into the center of the circle (**8 total**).
All good children go to heaven	Repeat above step moving out of the circle (**8 total**).
	FIGURE II
Pennies on the Ocean	Side-close, side-touch into circle (**4 total**).
Tuppence on the sea	Repeat above, moving out of circle (**4 total**).
Thruppence on the round-about and round goes she (he).	Two-hand or R. elbow turn CW with partner, 4 walking steps or 4 step-hops (**8 total**).

Repeat figure II.

NOTE: "The words 'tuppence,' and 'thruppence' are terms referring to English coins equal to two or three pennies or pence. When England converted its money into the decimal point system, the sum of two pennies was abbreviated as '2p' or 'two pence' shortened to 'tuppence,' and '3p' or 'three pence' can be shortened to 'thruppence.' The roundabout is a merry-go-round."[5]

SOURCES: Kathy Torrey, *Roots of the Tree of Life,* album, 4; Dudley Laufman, *Traditional Barn Dances* (Champaign: Human Kinetics, 2009), 152–53.

All Good Children

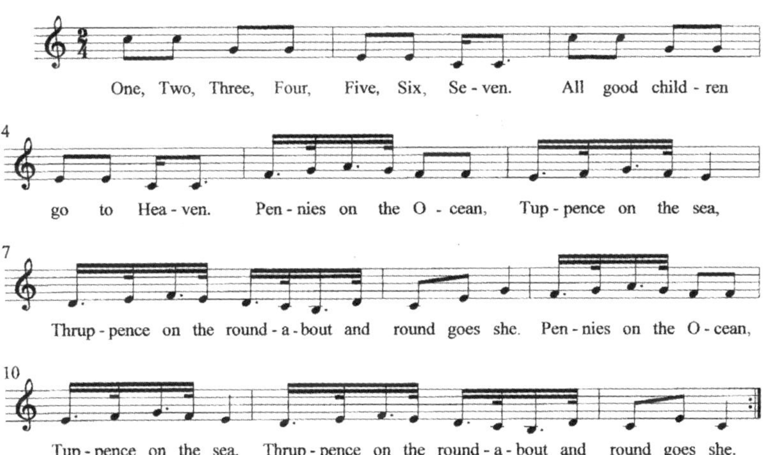

Notes for Five Children's Song Dances

1. LOST AND FOUND IN THE MIDDLE: Dancers who have lost their partners in the shuffle congregate in the middle to find a new partner.

2. In the process of spinning yarn, the machine that wound and measured the yarn was called a "weasel." Every thousand yards, this machine would make a popping sound, thus "Pop! goes the weasel."

3. "Pop Goes the Weasel," *Capering and Kickery*, last modified February 2009, www.kickery.com/2008/08/pop-goes-the-we .html.

4. Cory Webster, *Down in Utah*, audio cassette, 1995.

5. Dudley Laufman, *Traditional Barn Dances* (Champaign: Human Kinetics, 2009), 153.

MORE CHALLENGING DANCES

The Money Musk[1]

This dance was enjoyed by the Mormon Saints in Illinois and Utah. One Nauvoo sister recorded in her diary having "danced with Bro. Brigham, the Money Musk," at a dance held in the Nauvoo Council House.[2] Money Musk was most popular in Brigham City, Utah, in 1853.[3] In 1860 it appeared on the program of President Lincoln's Inaugural Ball.[4] This dance that is over two hundred years old is still danced in its original New England home with great fondness and enthusiasm.

The Dance

FORMATION: Longways sets, in triple minor proper formation (three couples working together, #1 couple, of the three, is active). (See Progression in Triple Minor Contras in Glossary.)

STEP: Walking

MUSIC: 32-bar "Money Musk," a Scottish tune specific to this dance.

A1 8 bars — ONCE AND A HALF AROUND: Couple #1 turns R. hands once and halfway around to go behind and below one couple, in between 2 and 3 couples where they are now in opposite gender lines. Twos move up (**16 total**).

A2 4 bars — BALANCE: Holding hands, lines of three walk forward 4 and back 4 (8).

4 bars — THREE QUARTERS ROUND: Couple #1 turns R. hands 3/4 around (8) into the middle, making two lines of three with couples #2 and #3, facing up and down the set (8) (**16 total**).

B1 4 bars — BALANCE: Lines of three walk forward 4 and back 4 (8).

4 bars	THREE QUARTERS ROUND: Couple #1 turns R. hands 3/4 around (8) to end up facing across the set in same gender lines between couples #2 and #3 (**16 total**).
B2 8 bars	RIGHT AND LEFT: Couples #1 and #2 cross over passing R. shoulders with opposite person, then pivot CCW, inside shoulders together, (L. person walks back and R. person walks forward) (8). Return in the same manner (**16 total**).

SOURCES: David Smuckler and David Millstone, *Cracking Chestnuts* (Haydenville: Country Dance & Song Society, 2008), 41; Rickey Holden, *The Contra Dance Book* (Newark: American Squares, 1956), 83–84; Henry Ford, *Good Morning* (Dearborn: Dearborn Publishing, 1945), 88–89.

Money Musk

American Traditional

The Tempest

This New England contra dance has an unusual "adapted double contra formation," which makes it interesting and fun to perform, lending variety to longways set dancing.[5] This dance has continued to survive and thrive in New England for many generations and was brought from New England to the West by the Mormon pioneers.[6] The name, "Tempest," was supposed to be chosen to describe the stormy effect of this unusual formation that's twice the size of a typical contra dance.[7]

The Dance

FORMATION: Two couples (the ones) face down the set, side-by-side, in a line of four. They start in between two couples (the twos), who are facing across the set with their partners to their sides. The ones dance with the twos closest to them in the long line, and progress down to the next set of twos on the sides.

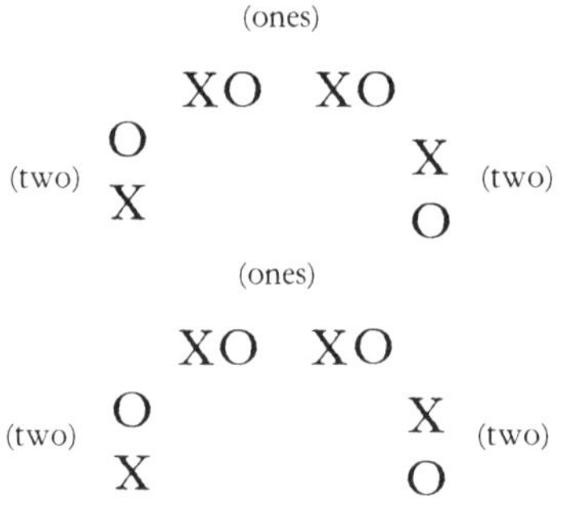

```
                (ones)
             XO      XO
       O                   X
(two)                          (two)
       X                   O
                (ones)
             XO      XO
       O                   X
(two)                          (two)
       X                   O
```

SET-UP: This formation is most easily set up by forming squares up and down the hall. Then have couple #2 (becomes #1) stand to the left of couple #1, facing down the hall, four in line.

Couples 3 and 4 (of quadrille numbering) stay in place and become twos.

STEPS: Walking

MUSIC: "The Tempest"

A1 8 bars	DOWN THE CENTER: First couples walk down the center, four in line (6), then each turn CCW as a couple (2) to return and face the side couples nearest their original positions (**16 total**).
A2 8 bars	CIRCLE FOUR: Ones circle four with these couples, 8 to the left, and 8 back to the right (**16 total**).
B1 8 bars	Ladies chain over and back (gent lead lady around with L. hand) (**16 total**).
B2 8 bars	HALF PROMENADE ACROSS: Half Right and Left back: Ones again forming a line of four to dance the next sequence by progressing down the center and back, to dance with the next set of twos (**16 total**).

PROGRESSION: The twos left out at the top wait one sequence, then turn to from a line of four to become ones. When the ones reach the bottom of the set, they separate and move to each side, becoming the new twos. All the twos need to move up the set while ones are going down the center and back.

SOURCES: David Smuckler and David Millstone, *Cracking Chestnuts* (Haydenville: Country Dance & Song Society, 2008), 64; Douglas Kennedy, *Community Dance Manual* (London: English Folk Dance and Song Society, 1967), 74.

The Tempest

Irish Traditional

Danish Waltz

(Also Danish Tucker, Tucker Waltz, or Spat Waltz)

I originally learned this dance from Clinton Peterson, who claimed this dance came across the plains with his Danish pioneer ancestors. Names and tunes for this dance vary by Utah region.

The Dance

FORMATION: Couples begin the dance with a waltz turn in ballroom position for part A, then walk side-by-side in a double circle, for part B. In the center of the circle is the "tucker," or extra man without a partner. Larger groups will likely have multiple tuckers.

STEPS: Walk (or march) and couple turning waltz

MUSIC: "Spat Waltz" (tune by Pattie Richards)

A 16 bars — COUPLE WALTZ TURN: Couples dance 8 CCW waltz turns in ballroom position, moving forward LOD. This couple turn can be substituted with a back-to-back/face-to-face figure as in Oslo Waltz (8) CCW and (8) CW.

B 16 bars — MARCH AND SPAT: The music changes to a 2/4 march, and couples walk forward, side-by-side LOD, lady on the right, holding inside hands.[8] Meanwhile the tucker begins to "spat" for a partner by walking up to a couple, clapping his hands (on count 1) at the gent, and taking his partner. This displaced gent rolls back CCW to "spat" the gent behind and steal his partner. And so on it goes like dominos around the circle, until the waltz music begins again, and couples resume the couple waltz turn with a new tucker in the center.

The last gent to be "spat" becomes the new tucker in the middle to start the dance over again.

SOURCES: I first learned this dance in 1983 from Clinton Petersen of Loa, Utah. Clinton and his brother, Clifton, (Clint and Cliff) had a band that played for dances down around Loa and Koosharem, Utah, near Capitol Reef National Park. The Petersen Brothers' Band also played for the yearly Koosharem Old Folks Day festival, where folks danced the old-time dances; Craig R. Miller, *An Old-Time Utah Dance Party* (Salt Lake City: Utah Arts Council, 2000), 59; Clinton Peterson, interview by author, Loa, UT, April 1983.

Spat Waltz

Utah Traditional

Opera Reel

The Opera Reel is mentioned many times in the Daughters of Utah Pioneers Museum archives and various other mid-nineteenth-century documents. It is another longways set, like the Virginia Reel, where only the couples at the top are active. This version is a very simple, fun introduction to early nineteenth-century longways sets.

The Dance

FORMATION: Longways set is "proper," with ladies on one side and gents on the other. The sets should be small—about four to six couples—to keep it interesting, since only the top two couples are active, and the remaining couples are inactive until it becomes their turn at the top of the set.

STEPS: Walking and Chassez

MUSIC: "Opera Reel" (specific to the dance)

A1 4 bars BALANCE: The top couple walks forward 4 and back 4.

4 bars CHASSEZ TO THE BOTTOM. Top couple join two hands and Chassez to the bottom of the set (**16 total**) (set moves up one position on 5-6-7-8).

A2 8 bars BALANCE AND CHASSEZ TO THE BOTTOM: The second couple repeats above figure (**16 total**).

B1 8 bars RIGHT AND LEFT: The two couples at the bottom cross over, passing R. shoulders with opposite (4) and pivot halfway around CCW shoulder-to-shoulder (4), and return in the same fashion (**16 total**).

B2 4 bars COUPLES 1 AND 2 CHASSEZ UP THE CENTER: Both couples at the bottom join two hands to Chassez up to their original positions (8).

4 bars FIRST COUPLE CAST OFF down the outside, to the bottom of the set (**16 total**).

REPEAT: The second couple now becomes the first couple, and the dance starts over again.

NOTE: A contemporary variation has all six couples in a set dancing during B1 (Right and Left Through). The two couples at the top circle left and right while the middle two do a R.- and L.-Hand Star (hands across).

SOURCES: Rickey Holden, *The Contra Dance Book* (Newark: American Squares, 1956), 83–84; Elias Howe, *American Dancing Master and Ballroom Prompter* (Boston: Miles & Dillingham Printers, 1866), 87.

Ninepin Quadrille

(Tucker Quadrille)

The tradition of having an extra man—called the "ninepin" or "tucker"—in the center of a circle or square, poised to cut-in, was very popular in pioneer times. There is a diary reference to "Tucker Quadrille," in Manti, Utah, which most likely refers to this enjoyable nineteenth-century quadrille mixer.[9] Other tucker dances in this collection include the Danish waltz (aka the Tucker waltz), Old Dan Tucker, and the children's dance: Somebody's Waiting.

FORMATION: Four couples in a quadrille, or square, with a ninepin in the center of the square. The couples are numbered as in a quadrille.

STEPS: Walking and Chassez

MUSIC: Jig medley: "The Irish Washerwoman," "Gary Owen," "Go to the Devil and Shake Yourself"

The Dance

A1 8 bars — HEAD CHASSEZ ACROSS AND BACK: First and second couples join two hands and Chassez across the set, passing with gent's back to the ninepin in the center (8). Then, keeping this position, they turn and Chassez back to place (8) (**16 total**).

A2 8 bars — SIDES CHASSEZ ACROSS AND BACK: Third and fourth couples do the same (**16 total**).

B1 8 bars — HEADS CIRCLE FOUR: The head couples move to the center and join hands four, circling left around the ninepin (8), then right (8) (**16 total**).

B2 8 bars — SIDES CIRCLE FOUR: Third and fourth couple do the same as above (**16 total**).

NINEPIN SWINGS EACH LADY WHILE GENTS TO THE CENTER AND CIRCLE: The ninepin, starting with couple #1, Two-Hand

Swings #1 lady, sending the #1 gent into the center. Then nine-pin goes to the #3 couple and Two-Hand Swings the #2 lady, sending the #3 gent into circle left with #1 gent. Ninepin continues in this fashion, swinging the remaining ladies, two and four, until all four gents are circling in the center. Ninepin then joins the gent's circle. The music suddenly stops, (or the caller, or ninepin, yells something like "Swing a partner!") and all the gents, including the ninepin, scramble to swing a lady partner at her home place. The leftover gent then becomes the ninepin, and the dance starts over again.

SOURCES: Aunt Carrie's *Popular Pastimes for Field and Fireside,* 142*; Dick's Caller Book*, 43; Eloise Hubbard Linscott, *Folk Songs of Old New England.* (New York: Dover Publications, Inc., 1993), 99–101.

I've chosen to feature the modern version of ninepin since it's easier to teach than the nineteenth-century version, which takes a goodly amount of time for the gents to learn skill of calling and intercepting a partner. For a challenge, try both!

Pioneer Era Version

In the mid-nineteenth century, this dance was a quadrille with one gentleman in the center as the ninepin, who randomly calls the following typical figures.

All Circle Left and Right; Forward Four (heads or sides/8-count balance); Ladies Chain (heads or sides); Ladies to the Center and Back; Gents to the Center and Back; Grand Right and Left.

On the Grand Right and Left, the ninepin gives a signal, such as clapping his hands or calling "Promenade" where he can cut in and take a partner leaving out one gent to become the nine-pin the next time around. This can also happen on any other figure where the lady is separated from her partner.

SOURCES: CDSS *Community Dance Manual*, 50.

The Irish Washerwomen

Irish Traditional

Gary Owen

Irish Traditional

Go to the Devil and Shake Yourself

American Traditional

Den Toppede Høne

(The Crested Hen)

The Crested Hen is a Danish trio dance: One man with two ladies. The Mormon pioneers enjoyed this threesome grouping in many other dances such as Scotch reel, threesome turning waltz, and the "double quadrille." The "crested hen" refers to the red stocking caps with tassels worn by Danish men, representing the rooster's comb. When the gent ducks under the arch in part B, the ladies each try to pull the cap off the gent's head to wear it. The lady who succeeds then becomes "the crested hen."

The Dance

FORMATION: One man between two ladies scattered around the floor or in a circle. To begin with, each threesome joins hands in their own individual circle.

STEP: Step-hop

MUSIC: "The Crested Hen"—a 2/4 tune specific to this dance.

A1 8 bars — STEP-HOP CIRCLE LEFT: They begin on the L. foot with a stamp-hop, and take 6 more step-hops CW around the circle. On the last measure, they jump on both feet, and hop on the L. foot to turn halfway around to face the opposite direction.

A2 8 bars — STEP-HOP CIRCLE RIGHT: Beginning with R. foot, and continue 8 step-hops CCW around the circle ending with the women dropping joined hands and moving back into a straight line with the gent.

B1 8 bars — RIGHT LADY UNDER ARCH: Lady on the right dances 4 step-hops under the arch formed by the gent and woman on the left, who step-hops in place. The gent follows R. lady under the arch

	to assume their original positions. Left Lady Under Arch: The above figure is repeated in reverse by the lady on the left.
B2 8 bars	Repeat B1.

(The band plays with the tempo to test the skill and endurance of the dancers. The dancers in the threesome circle should lean away strongly from each other with arms outstretched, giving weight to the circle in order to gain speed.)

VARIATIONS: On the beginning step-hops in the circle, two threesomes can combine. It can also be danced with several threesomes in one big single circle as a nice finale.

SOURCES: Anne Duggan, Jeanette Schlottman, and Abbie Rutledge, *Folk Dances of Scandinavia* (New York: A. S. Barnes, 1948), 49–50; Pittman and Waller Harris, *Dance a While*, 193; Elizabeth Burchenal, *Folk Dances of Denmark* (New York: G. Schirmer, 1915), 49.

Old Dan Tucker

Old Dan Tucker was one of the most popular tunes among the Mormon pioneers. In this dance, the "tucker" refers to the poor, unlucky fellow in the center who must cut in next to gain a partner, causing another gent to be expelled and become the next tucker. Dancers with partners often taunt and tease the tucker, all in fun.

FORMATION: A circle of six to twelve couples with an extra man or two in the center as the tucker(s). The larger the circle, the more tuckers are needed.

STEPS: Brisk walking, balance, and Chassez

MUSIC: "Old Dan Tucker," "Over the Waterfall"

The Dance

A 8 bars	BALANCE/TURN CORNER/PARTNER (Verse): All join hands and balance to the tucker. (Step right-hop, while swinging left across front, repeat on left side.) (4) Turn corner once with the R. hand (6), then partner once around with the L. hand (6) (**16 total**).
B 8 bars	GRAND CHAIN (Chorus): Pull partner by with the right for a Grand Chain (Grand Right and Left), gents go CCW, ladies CW. This is where the tucker cuts in, expelling an extra gent to be the next tucker (**16 total**).
A 8 bars	PROMENADE (Verse): Gents take the nearest lady to promenade CCW (**16 total**). (Lost and found in the middle: anyone who's lost their partner comes to the middle to find a new partner.)
B 8 bars	BALANCE TO THE CENTER/CHASSEZ (Chorus): All join hands and balance forward 4 and back 4. Keeping hold of hands, all Chassez left (8) CW (**16 total**).

SONG

VERSE

Old Dan Tucker's a fine old man,
Washed his face in a frying pan,
Combed his hair with a wagon wheel,
And died with a tooth-ache in his heel.

CHORUS

Git out of the way for Old Dan Tucker,
He's too late to git his supper,
Supper's over and breakfast a-cookin',
An' Old Dan Tucker's standin' a-lookin'.

SOURCE: Elizabeth Burcehnal, *American Country Dances* vol. 1 (New York: G. Schirmer, 1915), 62.

Old Dan Tucker

American Traditional

Over the Waterfall

American Traditional

Miss McLeod's Reel

Here is another traditional New England contra dance brought across the plains by the pioneers. It was most likely included in the category of Scotch reels, often referred to by the Utah pioneers. According to legendary New England caller, Ralph Page, "Like the Scots themselves, reels are energetic pieces, guaranteed sure cures for everything from the blues to poor circulation."[10]

The Dance

FORMATION: Longways sets of six to eight couples, duple proper. Actives are 1, 3, 5, etc.

STEP: Walking

MUSIC: "Miss McLeod's Reel"

A1 8 bars	DOWN THE CENTER/CAST OFF: Actives down the center (6) and turn as a couple (2) to return (8). Actives cast around the inactive couples to face across the set while 2s move up (The set is now improper) (**16 total**).
A2 8 bars	Ladies chain and back with this couple above (**16 total**).
B1 4 bars	All half promenade across the set (8).
4 bars	All Half Right and Left back to place (**16 total**).
B2 8 bars	BALANCE/ACTIVES CROSS BACK: Everyone forward 4 and back 4, holding hands along the lines. Lines forward again, active couples crossing back with quick face-to-face CW turn in the middle, and all back up to place (**16 total**).

Repeat as many times as desired. When inactive couples reach the top of the set, they become active and vice versa with the active couples at the bottom of the set.

SOURCES: Rickey Holden, *The Contra Dance Book* (Newark: American Squares, 1956), 83.

Miss McLeod's Reel

American Traditional

Fisher's Hornpipe

This is an early American contra dance from the late 1700s. The Fisher's Hornpipe tune appears in many accounts of Mormon pioneers dancing.[11] This dance is another New England "Chestnut" contra dance—a very old and traditional classical dance. As in the Money Musk, it has the "triple minor" formation (three couples working together rather than two, as in the "duple" formation). This triple formation was most common in early contra dances, but is rarely seen today in contemporary contra dances, especially in the Western United States.

The Dance

FORMATION: Longways set, triple minor proper. The #1s, or active couples, work their way down the set, while the 2s and 3s move up, changing alternately from 2 to 3, and back, as they progress up the set. (See Progression for Triple Minor Contras in Glossary.)

STEP: Walking

MUSIC: "Fisher's Hornpipe"—a very popular fiddle tune of the same name.

A1 8 bars — DOWN THE OUTSIDE AND BACK: Active couple cast off down the outside of the set, and back (**16 total**).

A2 8 bars — DOWN THE CENTER AND BACK TO CAST OFF: Active couple dance down the center, turning alone (2), and back to cast off around the second couple, progressing down one place between the 2s and 3s (**16 total**).

B1 8 bars — HANDS ACROSS: Active couple stars R. hands across with couple 3 below (8) and stars L. hands across back with couple 2 above (**16 total**).

B2 8 bars RIGHT AND LEFT THROUGH: Couple one does a Right and Left Through across and back with the couple 2 above, passing R. shoulders with the opposite (4) and rotating CCW halfway, shoulder to shoulder (person on the L. goes back while person on the R. goes forward) (4) CCW to return the same manner (**16 total**).

Having progressed down one position, the active couples begin the dance again with the couple below, which are now the new 2s, and the new third couple.

(This is the period-correct version. It can also be done in duple formation, which may be more comfortable for contemporary contra dancers.)

B1 ALTERNATIVE: Circle six: All three couples take hands six to circle left (8) and right back to place (**8 total**).

SOURCES: Rickey Holden, *The Contra Dance Book* (Newark: American Squares, 1956), 62; David Smuckler and David Millstone, *Cracking Chestnuts* (Haydenville: Country Dance & Song Society, 2008), 69; Eloise Hubbard Linscott, *Folk Songs of Old New England.* (New York: Dover Publications, Inc., 1993), 76–77.

Fisher's Hornpipe

American Traditional

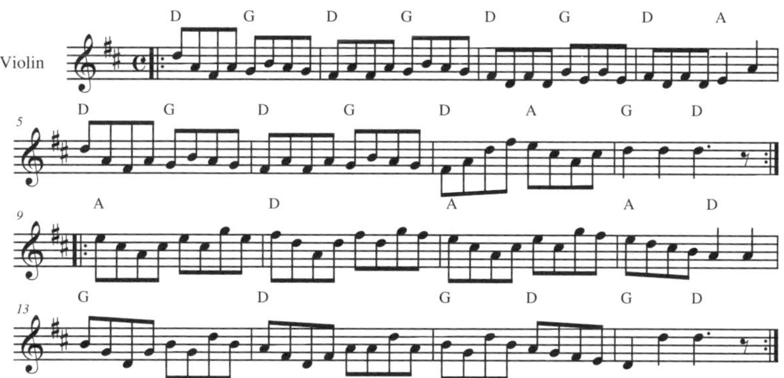

Sir Roger de Coverley

The Sir Roger de Coverley is an English ancestor of the Virginia Reel. The Sir Roger de Coverley was popular in the United States during the Revolutionary Era. When George Washington held dances at Mt. Vernon, they always closed with this, his favorite dance.[12] Sir Roger de Coverley was also featured at Feziwig's Ball in Charles Dickens's *A Christmas Carol*. In 1862, Brigham Young organized a group to dance Sir Roger de Coverley at a Christmas Eve party at the Salt Lake Theater.[13]

The Dance

FORMATION: Longways sets up to nine couples facing, gents on one side and ladies on the other. Five couple sets seem to do best at keeping with the phrases of the music.

STEP: Walking or skipping, one step per count.

MUSIC: "Sir Roger de Coverley," "Andrew Carey," "Rakes of Westmeath," "Hyp Doctor." Slip-jig medley.

A 8 bars — FORWARD AND BACK: Top lady and bottom gent go through the center of the set to meet each other and salute (6), and back to place (6).

Top gent and bottom lady the same (**24 total**).

B 8 bars — RIGHT-HAND TURN: Top lady and bottom gent meet in the center to turn R. hands around and back to place (12).

Top gent and bottom lady the same (**24 total**).

C 8 bars — LEFT-HAND TURN: Top lady and bottom gent meet in the center to turn L. hands around and back to place (12).

Top gent and bottom lady the same (**24 total**).

A 8 bars — TWO-HAND TURN: Top lady and bottom gent meet in the center to turn two hands around CW and back to place (12).

Top lady and bottom gent the same (**24 total**).

B 8 bars — DOS-A-DOS: Top gent and bottom lady meet in the center, Dos-a-Dos and back to place (12).

Top lady and bottom gent do the same (**24 total**).

C 8 bars — Top Couple Chassez to the Bottom and Back (**24 or less**).

Figure 1: Lace the Boot

The top couple cross over, passing R. shoulders, to cast down the outside between the second and third couples and cross again passing L. shoulders, and so on down the set. They pass alternate shoulders across the set, always keeping lady closest to the bottom of the set during the cross over. At the bottom of the set, they take two hands and chassez to the top of the set.

Figure 2: Walk the Highway

Top couple separate, going down the outside of the set, gents line follows #1 gent, and ladies follow #1 lady (like peeling a banana). Top couple meets at the bottom and lead the couples up to reform the set. Top couple then Chassez to the bottom of the set, and the dance starts over with a new top couple.

NOTE: These last two figures tend to go over the phrase of the music, especially when there are more than five couples in a set. The caller needs to hold the prompt to start the dance until the beginning of a phrase, if possible, keeping in mind the momentum and flow of the dance. This whole dance is often danced un-phrased without prompts when the dancers have the figures memorized.

SOURCES: Aunt Carrie, *Popular Pastimes for Field and Fireside*, 1867, 141–42; Barbara Menard Pugliese, Medford (Boston), MA, *Recreating the Nineteenth Century Ballroom*, blogspot, recreating19cballroom.blogspot.com, November 21, 2012.

Sir Roger De Coverly

English Traditional

Andrew Carey

Irish Traditional

Rakes of Westmeath

Irish Traditional

Hyp Doctor

Irish Traditional

Twin Sisters

In 1852, Twin Sisters—along with the Money Musk—was the most popular dance in Brigham City, Utah.[14] Twin Sisters has been included in many traditional dance collections up into the 1950s and beyond. It has been danced as a polka, a waltz, and its formation has been known by many other names.[15]

The Dance

FORMATION: Longways sets, duple proper of about six couples.

STEPS: Walking and Chassez

MUSIC: "Land O' Sweet Erin"

A1 8 bars LADIES CHASSEZ ACROSS AND BACK: Active ladies and inactive ladies turn face, take two hands to Chassez 8 across the set, between their partners, and 8 back. Simultaneously, the gents face and Chassez across the set, and back on the outside of their partners (**16 total**).

A2 8 bars GENTS AND LADIES CHASSEZ ACROSS AND BACK: Gents take two hands and Chassez 8 across and 8 back between their partners while ladies do the same on the outside of their partners (**16 total**).

B1 8 bars ACTIVES DOWN THE CENTER AND BACK/CAST OFF: Actives walk down the center (6), turn individually so still proper (2), then up the set (4) to cast around the inactives (4) into second place to progress (**16 total**).

B2 8 bars RIGHT AND LEFT: These two couples cross over passing R. shoulders with opposite, then pivot CCW, inside shoulders together, (L. person walks backward and R. person walks forward) (8). Return in the same manner (**16 total**).

Repeat with one or two couples waiting out at the top and/or bottom of the set to come back in as new ones and twos.

SOURCES: Elias Howe, *American Dancing Master and Ballroom Prompter* (Boston: Miles & Dillingham Printers, 1866), 99; Rickey Holden, *The Contra Dance Book* (Newark: American Squares, 1956), 99.

Land O' Sweet Erin

The Scotch Reel

Here is another trio dance, with one man dancing with two ladies.[16] The original description of this dance closely resembles the English dance, "Three Meet."[17] It also resembles the "Swedish Dance" described in mid-nineteenth century dance manuals.[18] This choreography is a combination of the above dances created to fit the musical phrase.

The Dance

FORMATION: Each gentleman is holding hands with two ladies, one on each side, facing another trio. Multiple trios can form a triple Sicilian circle around the room. If there are six trios, or less, they can form a longways set and progress as in a contra dance.

OO OO OO
XX XX XX
OO OO OO

STEPS: Brisk walking

MUSIC: "Scotch Reel"

A1 8 bars GENTS TURN THEIR LADIES: Gents turn the lady on their right once around CW with an elbow swing (8). Gents then L. elbow swing their L. hand lady once around CCW (**16 total**).

A2 8 bars CIRCLE THREE: Gents circle three once around CW with the two ladies on their right (their partner and opposite lady on their right diagonal) (8). Then gents lead off to circle CCW with left partner and the opposite trio lady on their left diagonal (**16 total**).

B1 8 bars FORWARD AND TURN: Gents link arms with both their partners and walk 4 steps forward to meet the other trio as they rotate quarter CCW. Then both trios continue rotating quarter CCW to back up into opposite's position (8). They repeat this same figure, continuing to rotate CCW to return to original positions (**16 total**).

B2 8 bars BALANCE AND PASS THROUGH: Holding hands, trios walk forward 4 and back 4. All drop hands in their line to pass through (8) (passing R. shoulders with opposite person) on to next trio (**16 total**).

Repeat with this next trio, and on through the circle or set. The trio expelled at the top or bottom of the set turns halfway to face back into the set, and waits out one sequence, as in a contra dance.

SOURCES: Ruth E. Yashko, "An Historical Study of Pioneer Dancing in Utah," (master's thesis, University of Utah, 1947), 36; Douglas Kennedy, *Community Dance Manual* (London: English Folk Dance and Song Society, 1967), 43; Thomas Hillgrove, *A Complete Practical Guide to the Art of Dancing* (New York: Dick & Fitzgerald, 1867), 228–29.

Scotch Reel

American Traditional

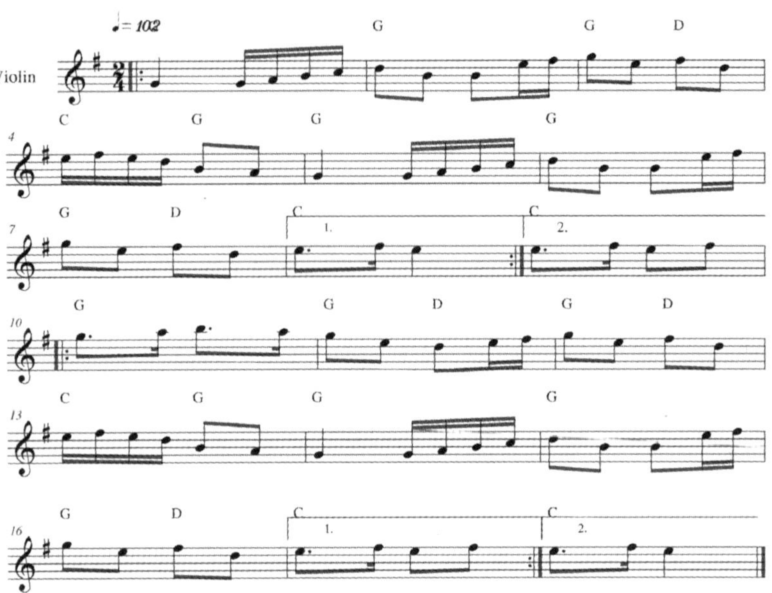

French Four[19]

French Four is a very old traditional contra dance, included in the New England "Chestnuts" collection, along with Money Musk, The Tempest, and Fisher's Hornpipe. It was mentioned in several accounts of the dancing in the Nauvoo Temple, prior to the dedication,[20] and in Colonel Kane's account of the Farewell Ball held to send off the Mormon Battalion.[21]

The Dance[22]

FORMATION: Longways sets, duple proper

STEP: Walking

MUSIC: "Mason's Apron"/"Speed the Plow" medley

A1 4 bars — ACTIVES BALANCE: Number one active couple balances forward 4 and back 4 (8).

4 bars — ACTIVES CROSS OVER AND DOWN: Active couples cross over passing R. shoulders, down outside of the set, below one couple who moves up (8) (**16 total**).

A2 8 bars — BALANCE AND CROSS BACK: Active couples balance, forward (4) and back (4), and cross over again, passing R. shoulders, to walk up the outside back to place, while the inactives move back down (**16 total**).

B1 8 bars — DOWN THE CENTER AND BACK/CAST OFF: Actives walk down the center (6), and back up the set to cast off around inactive couple. Twos move up (**16 total**).

B2 8 bars — RIGHT AND LEFT: Active couples cross over passing R. shoulders with opposite, then pivot CCW, inside shoulders together, (L. person walks backward and R. person walks forward) (8). Return in the same manner (**16 total**).

SOURCES: Rickey Holden, *The Contra Dance Book* (Newark: American Squares, 1956), 63; David Smuckler and David Millstone, *Cracking Chestnuts* (Haydenville: Country Dance & Song Society, 2008), 69; Eloise Hubbard Linscott, *Folk Songs of Old New England.* (New York: Dover Publications, Inc., 1993), 77–78.

French Four #2

(Contemporary Version) Duple Proper

A1 Active couples take hands and balance (4 count forward and back), cross the set, passing R. shoulders, to go down the outside below the twos, who move up (8). Actives balance again (4), cross the set and go up the outside to original place while twos move down (8) **(16 total)**.

A2 Actives balance and swing in the middle (**16 total**).

B1 Actives down the center turning as a couple (proper) (8). Actives return and cast off (arms around back) (8) **(16 total)**.

B2 Right and Left Through, over and back (proper) (**16 total**).

Mason's Apron

American Traditional

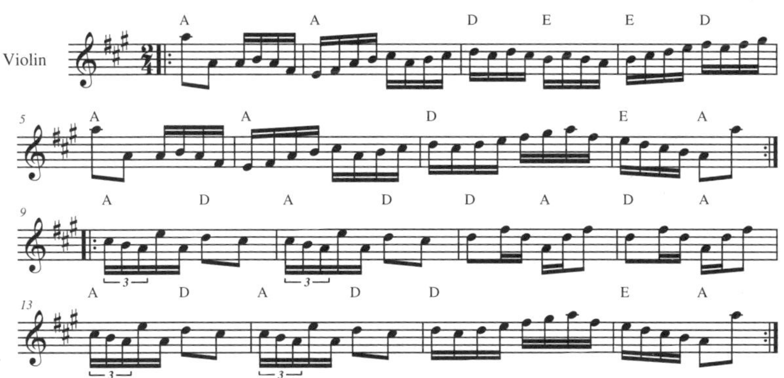

Speed the Plow

American Traditional

Notes for More Challenging Dances

1. This is the nineteenth-century 32-bar version. During the twentieth century it decreased to its currently popular, speedier form of 24 bars: A1, A2, B1. Henry Ford, *Good Morning* (Dearborn: Dearborn Publishing, 1945), 88.

2. Kenneth W. Godfrey, Audrey M. Godfrey, and Jill Mulvay Derr, *Women's Voices: An Untold History of the Latter-Day Saints* (Salt Lake City: Desert Book Co., 1982), 179.

3. Levi Edgar Young, *The Founding of Utah* (New York: Charles Scribner's Sons, 1923), 329.

4. Phil and Vivian Williams, *Dances of the Oregon Trail* (Seattle: Voyager Recordings, 2000), CD.

5. David Smuckler and David Millstone, *Cracking Chestnuts* (Haydenville: Country Dance & Song Society, 2008), 64.

6. Included on a dance bill list in Daughters of the Utah Pioneers Museum archives.

7. Eloise Hubbard Linscott, *Folk Songs of Old New England* (New York: Dover Publications, Inc., 1993), 113.

8. This part may also be performed in varsovienne position, with ladies still on the right, their hands held up in a *W*, and gents on the left holding both of the ladies' hands.

It helps to have the gents practice the "spatting" part of the dance to the count of "one, two," clapping only on count one, then practicing it with music. (In a Norwegian version of this dance, the gents spat quickly so as to be guaranteed a partner.)

9. Diary of Bonnie Romney's 2nd great-grandfather, Fred Neilsen, of Manti, Utah.

10. Beth Tolman and Ralph Page, *The Country Dance Book* (Brattleboro: Stephen Greene Press, 1976), 111.

11. In reference to the dancing in the Nauvoo Temple in 1846 prior to the pioneer trek West, William Clayton recorded the following in his journal:

> After the regular exercises and business of the day was over, and the meetings of the High Council and the High Priests were closed, we have some excellent instrumental and vocal music. Several members of the Band having been invited by Elder Kimball, viz; Wm. Pitt, Wm. Clayton, J. F. Hutchinson, and James Smithies. They performed several beautiful pieces of music and at the request of Joseph Young, played Fishers Hornpipe, upon which brother Joseph broke the gravity of the scene by dancing a hornpipe by himself. He was soon joined by John L. Butler, Ezra T. Benson and A[lbert] P. Rockwood. These danced until they were weary and sat down.

William Clayton, *An Intimate Chronicle, The Journals of William Clayton*, ed. George D. Smith (Salt Lake City: Signature Books, 1955): 250.

12. Vivian and Phil Williams, *Fiddle Tunes of the Lewis and Clark Era* (Seattle: Voyager Recording, 2002), CD.

13. Susan A. Madsen, *Christmas, A Joyful Heritage* (Salt Lake City: Deseret Book, 1984).

"President Young then surprised the group by signaling the orchestra members. They started to play 'Sir Roger de Coverley.' President Young and a selected group danced this popular English dance. The remainder of the time was spent dancing, and all had an opportunity to enjoy themselves." "Yule Celebration Richer with Echo From Pioneers," *Deseret News*, December 1982.

14. Young, *The Founding of Utah*, 392.

15. Rickey Holden, *The Contra Dance Book* (Newark: American Squares, 1956), 99.

16. Ruth E. Yashko, "An Historical Study of Pioneer Dancing in Utah," (master's thesis, University of Utah, 1947), 36.

17. Douglas Kennedy, *Community Dance Manual* (London: English Folk Dance and Song Society, 1967), 43.

18. Thomas Hillgrove, *A Complete Practical Guide to the Art of Dancing* (New York: Dick & Fitzgerald, 1867), 228–29.

19. Many pioneer accounts may have used the term "French fours" in reference to the quadrille or cotillion formation of four couples in a square, as in "French fours would form a cotillion and dance until bedtime." Thomas L. Kane, quoted in Edward W. Tullidge, *History of Salt Lake City* (Salt Lake City: Star Printing Company, 1886), 31-32.

20. On December 30 1845, when the Saints were working on the Nauvoo Temple, Brigham Young recorded the following:

> The labors of the day having been brought to a close at so early and hour . . . it was thought proper to have a little season of recreation, accordingly Brother Hans Hanson was invited to produce his violin. He did so and played several lively airs, among the rest some were very good lively dancing tunes. This was too much for the gravity of Joseph Young, who indulged in a hornpipe, and was soon joined by several others, and before the dance was over several French fours were indulged in. The first was opened by myself. . . . The spirit of dancing increased until the whole floor was covered with dancers.

Brigham Young, as quoted by Cecil E. McGavin, *The Mormon Pioneers* (Salt Lake City: Stevens and Wells, Inc., 1947), 29–30.

21. In 1846, Colonel Thomas Kane also recorded observing the Mormon pioneers dancing the "French Fours" at the farewell ball held at Council Bluff prior to the Mormon Battalion's departure for California. Thomas L. Kane, quoted

in Edward W. Tullidge, *History of Salt Lake City* (Salt Lake City: Star Printing Company, 1886), 31–32.

22. Country Dance and Song Society, Inc., "Cracking Chestnuts: French Four Contra Dance," YouTube video, posted September 2013, video, www.youtube.com/watch?v=E8j1VFjN9qY.

ARCHIVAL DANCES

Marlbrouk Cotillion

It is only fitting to include this cotillion with some "fancy footwork," representing the style of dancing Brigham Young loved best. By the mid-nineteenth century, fancy footwork had gone out of style and was thought too show-offish and vulgar by fashionable ballrooms of the East, where quadrilles were danced with languorous walking and gliding elegance.[1] But Brother Brigham still loved the lively cotillion because it brought "sweat to the brow" and "vigor to the body."[2]

The Dance

FORMATION: A quadrille set of four couples, heads and sides.

STEPS: Chassez, balance, rigadoon, and walking

MUSIC: "Marlbrouk"[3]

CHANGE 1

A1 8 bars	All couples take hands in a circle of eight, balance, rigadoon (8), then Chassez (8) CCW halfway around the set (**16 total**).
A2 8 bars	All balance, rigadoon, then Chassez 8 back CW to place (**16 total**).

CHORUS

Refrain 4 bars	Head couples go forward 4 to meet and rigadoon, while the side couples stand (**8 total**).
A1 4 bars	Heads take two hands with the opposite to Chassez 4 out between the split side couples, and rigadoon. The side couples are simultaneously separating with 4 Chassez, ladies to the right and gents to the left, then rigadoon in place (**8 total**).

A2 4 bars — Head couples Chassez 4 back together in the center, and back up 4 steps into original place, while the sides Chassez 4 back together and rigadoon (**8 total**).

This 12-bar figure is repeated with the side couples commencing the figure, sides, and heads swapping movements.

This whole 24-bar figure is repeated as a chorus after all changes.

CHANGE 2

A1 8 bars — TURN PARTNERS: All couples face partners, balance, and rigadoon (8). Right-Hand Turn (8) with partners once around (this turn can also be done with arms crossed and L. and R. hands joined behind the back) (**16 total**).

A2 8 bars — Repeat above with Left-Hand Turn (**16 total**).

CHORUS

CHANGE 3

A1 8 bars — GRAND CHAIN: Partners face and, taking R. hands, L. with next, R. with the next halfway around to meet partner (12) and rigadoon (4) (**16 total**).

A2 8 bars — Continue Grand Chain around to meet partner again at home position (12) and rigadoon (4) (**16 total**).

CHORUS

CHANGE 4 (Repeat Change 1)

CHORUS AS FINALE

FANCY FOOTWORK (TWO TYPES OF BALANCE STEPS):

1. SIDE BALANCE:

Count 1: Step to the right on the R. foot.

Count 2: Close the L. foot to the R. foot without taking weight.

Counts 3 and 4: Repeat above to the left.

2. PAS DE BASQUE: Perform the balance step as above, only putting weight on the closing foot with the rhythm 1 and 2, 3 and 4. Closing foot takes the "and" count as in English and Scottish country dancing. The movement is a slightly bouncy, down-up-down.

3. RIGADOON STEP

Count 1: Small leap onto L. foot while extending R. foot out in 2nd position.

Count 2: Same as above with opposite footwork.

Count 3 and 4: Two small jumps on both feet.

"Dancing seems to be the considered and edifying exercise. The Prophet dances, the Apostles dance, and the Bishops dance. . . . [The dance] is not in the languid, done-up style that polite Europe affects, as in the days of our grandparents. 'Positions' are maintained, steps are elaborately executed, and a somewhat severe muscular exercise is the result.'"[4]

SOURCES

James E. Morrison, *Twenty-Four Early American County Dances, Cotillions & Reels for the Year 1976* (New York: The Country Dance Society, Inc., 1976), 50–51.

Marlbrouk

American Traditional

Violin

The Caledonian Quadrille

The Caledonian Quadrille first appeared in the United States during the 1820s. It is thought to have no direct Scottish connection but to be of English origin, danced to Scottish tunes. Dance notes for the Caledonian Quadrille are interpreted here from notes in the call book of H. P. Larsen.[5]

FORMATION: Four couples form a square or quadrille formation, ladies on the right of the gent. Heads are #1 and #2 (numbering across the set). Sides are #3 and #4.

STEPS: Walking, Chassez, and balance step.

MUSIC: Arrangement of "New Caledonian Quadrille"[6]

The Dance

Figure 1 (32 bars)

8-bar intro. Couples confer on the figure, then salute partner (16).

8 bars	RIGHT AND LEFT HANDS ACROSS: Head couples star right (8), and left back (8) (**16 total**).
8 bars	BALANCE/TWO-HAND TURN TO PLACE: Holding hands in a circle in the center all side balance twice (8). Partners two-hand CW turn to place (**16 total**).
8 bars	LADIES CHAIN: Head two ladies cross giving R. hands as they pass, and L. hands to the opposite

gent who leads them around to face into the set. Ladies return in same manner (**16 total**).

8 bars: HALF PROMENADE/HALF RIGHT AND LEFT: Head couples half promenade across (8), then right and left across back to place (**16 total**).

Sides perform above figure.

Figure 2 (24 bars)

15-count intro. Couples confer on the upcoming figure.

A FOUR LADIES BALANCE 4 forward and 4 back. Four gents balance 4 forward and 4 back (**16 total**).

B LADIES BALANCE/TWO-HAND SWING CORNERS: All four ladies balance to corner on (forward 4 and back 4) and Two-Hand Swing corner, ending up in corner's partner position (**16 total**).

C ALL PROMENADE WITH CORNER once around, returning to gent's home position (**16 total**).

Repeat above figure 3 more times so ladies return to their original partner.

Figure 3 (32 bars)
8-bar intro. Couples confer.

8 bars	HEADS BALANCE/TWO-HAND SWING OPPOSITE: Heads forward 4, back 4, forward to swing opposite once, and back to place (8) (**16 total**).
8 bars	DRAWERS: First couple passes between the second couple, separates, and returns on the outside, while second couple passes on the outside and returns between the first couple (**16 total**).
8 bars	CORNERS BALANCE/TWO-HAND SWING: All balance to corners (forward 4 and back 4). Two-Hand Swing corner once around to return to original position (**16 total**).
8 bars	ALL BALANCE TWICE: All join hands in a circle to walk forward 4 into the circle and back 4, twice (**16 total**).
	Heads repeat whole figure, reversing drawers with couple two commencing the figure by passing between couple one.
	Sides perform above figures.

Figure 4 (32 bars)
8-bar intro. Couples confer.

A1 8 bars	ADVANCE AND STOP: First lady advances and stops (4). Opposite gent advances and stops (4). Second lady advances and stops (4). Opposite gent advances and stops (4) (**16 total**).
A2 8 bars	BALANCE/TWO-HAND TURN: These couples turn to face partner and side balance twice, R.L., R.L. (8). Then heads Two-Hand Turn back to original positions (8) (**16 total**).

B1 8 bars — LADIES CROSS/GENTS CROSS: All four ladies cross over to their right to take corner's partner's place (4). All four gents cross over to the left to take their corner's partner's place (4). Repeat (8) (**16 total**).

B2 8 bars — HALF CIRCLE/TWO-HAND SWING: All join hands to circle CCW back to place (8). Two-Hand Swing partner (8) (**16 total**).

Sides perform above figure.

Figure 5 (40 bars—repeated by the side couples)

8-bar intro. Couples confer.

8 bars — HEADS PROMENADE slowly CCW once around inside the set (8 across, 8 return) (**16 total**).

8 bars — FOUR LADIES R. AND L. HANDS ACROSS: Ladies star right once around (8) and back with left (8), offering R. hand to partner's left to form large star figure, all facing CCW (**16 total**).

8 bars — ALL BALANCE/TWO-HAND SWING: All side balance the star twice, right, left, right, left (8) and Two-Hand Swing to place (8) (**16 total**).

10 bars — ALL SALUTE/GRAND CHAIN: All slowly salute partners (4 counts down, 4 counts up). Grand Right and Left. Halfway around to meet partner (12) (**20 total**).

6 bars — PROMENADE/LADIES CENTER: All promenade partner CCW to place (10). Gents lead ladies into center to face them (ladies back to center of quadrille) (2) (**12 total**).

8 bars — ALL CHASSEZ TO CORNERS/TWO-HAND SWING: All Chassez (4) to the right, away from partner to corners of the set and (4) back to partner.

Two-Hand Swing (8) once around to end (**16 total**).

Sides perform above figure ending with a final salute (bow and curtsy) to partner. Gents offer their arm to escort the lady off the dance floor.

BALANCE STEP, SCOTTISH STYLE: *Count One*: Step to the right with the R. foot. *And*: step on the L. foot next to the R. foot. *Count Two*: Step again on the R. foot in place (*And*) Hold. Reverse the footwork for *3 And 4* (*And*).

SOURCES: H. P. Larsen, *Pioneer Songs* (Salt Lake City: Daughters of Utah Pioneers, 1932), 276; *Dick's Quadrille Call-Book* (New York: Dick & Fitzgerald, Publishers, 1878), 56; Thomas Hillgrove, *A Complete Practical Guide to the Art of Dancing* (New York: Dick & Fitzgerald, 1867), 108; "New Caledonian Quadrille," *19th-Century American Sheet Music* (Boston: Oliver Ditson & Co., 1859), dc.lib.unc.edu/cdm/ref/collection/sheetmusic/id/30812.

Plain Quadrille

The Plain Quadrille was the most popular quadrille during the mid-nineteenth century. It is characterized by its "quiet, easy style, avoiding all show or affectation." The simplicity of the quadrille made it "adaptable to all classes. . . . The old, the young, the robust and the slender—all may mingle in its easy, pleasant evolutions with equal satisfaction."[7] The structure of the Plain Quadrille was often utilized for the Waltz Quadrille and Polka Quadrille, where the dancers would waltz or polka in place of walking.[8]

FORMATION: Four couples in a quadrille, or square, formation.

STEPS: Walking, chasse, and balance

MUSIC: An arrangement of "The Mormons: Quadrille"[9]

The Dance

Figure 1 (32 bars)

16-count intro. Partners salute (bow and curtsy), chat, and confer with each other on the figure.

8 bars	RIGHT AND LEFT: Head couples cross over, ladies between opposite couple, giving R. hands to opposite gent. The gent then takes his partner's L. hand to lead her halfway around to face into the set. Head couples return to their original position in the same fashion (**16 total**).
8 bars	PROMENADE ACROSS AND BACK: Head couples promenade across the set (gents passing L. shoulders) and return to place in the same fashion (**16 total**).
8 bars	LADIES' CHAIN: Head two ladies cross, giving R. hands as they pass and L. hands to the opposite gent. The two gents lead the two ladies around to face into the set (8). Repeat to return (**16 total**).

8 bars — HALF PROMENADE/HALF RIGHT AND LEFT: Head couples half promenade across, and Half Right and Left back (**16 total**).

Sides repeat above figure.

Figure 2: The Basket Figure (40 bars)

16-count intro.

4 bars — BALANCE: Heads walk forward 4 and back 4 (**8 total**).

4 bars — HALF RIGHT AND LEFT ACROSS: Head couples Half Right and Left across (**8 total**).

4 bars — TWO-HAND CHASSEZ ACROSS: Heads face their partner to take two hands and Chassez across the set back to place, ladies passing back-to-back in the center (**8 total**).

4 bars — BALANCE AND TURN PARTNER: Keeping the two-hand hold, head couples balance to each other (forward touch and back-touch), and Two-Hand Turn CW half-way around to place to open out and face center (**8 total**).

8 bars — FOUR LADIES CIRCLE: All four ladies join hands in the center of the set and circle (8) to the left, and (8) to the right, (**16 total**) pulling the circle in to stand close while . . .

8 bars — FOUR GENTS CIRCLE: All four gents join hands to circle left (6) around the ladies, turning back 7 and 8 (8). They walk 3 more counts to stand to the left of their partners and raise their joined hands up to hold on count 4 (while music slows with a fermata). In 4 counts the ladies move backward under the gents' joined hands, which the gents drop simultaneously in front of the ladies to form a basket (8) (**16 total**).

4 bars — ALL BALANCE FORWARD AND BACK: All balance the basket circle forward touch and back touch twice (**8 total**).

4 bars — TURN PARTNERS: All two-hand CW turn partners back to place (**8 total**).

Sides lead off to repeat above figure.

Figure 3 (32 bars)

16-count intro.

4 bars — HALF RIGHT AND LEFT: Head couples cross over, ladies in the middle, touching R. hands with the opposite in passing. The head gents then take their partners' L. hands to lead her around in a half left turn to face back into the set (**8 total**).

4 bars — LEFT HANDS BACK: Head couples return into the middle, with the ladies joining and retaining L. hands with opposite gent (4). Ladies then make a quarter turn to give their R. hands (crossed over their left) to their partners (**8 total**).

4 bars — BALANCE IN CENTER: The four dancers, holding hands in this formation, balance forward and back twice (**8 total**).

4 bars — PROMENADE TURN TO PLACE: All drop L. hands. Gents, retaining their partners' R. hands, assume promenade position and walk CCW all the way around (gents L. shoulder to L. shoulder) and back to place (**8 total**).

4 bars — TWO LADIES BALANCE: Head ladies walk forward 4 and back 4 (**8 total**).

4 bars — TWO GENTS BALANCE: Head gents walk forward 4 and back 4 (**8 total**).

4 bars	HEAD COUPLES BALANCE: Head couples walk forward 4 and back 4 (**8 total**).
4 bars	HALF RIGHT AND LEFT: Head couples Half Right and Left back to place (**8 total**).
	Sides repeat above figure.

Figure 4 (32 bars)

16-count intro.

4 bars	HEADS BALANCE: Head couples walk forward 4 and back 4 (**8 total**).
4 bars	FORWARD FOUR, FIRST LADY CROSS OVER: Head couples walk forward 4, and couple one lady crosses over to retire with second gent and partner, first gent retiring at same time alone to his place (**8 total**).
4 bars	FORWARD 3 AND BACK: The second gent and two ladies advance 4 steps and retire (**8 total**).
4 bars	FORWARD AGAIN AND LADIES CROSS OVER: The second gent again advances and hands the two ladies to the first gent (who has advanced to receive them). All retire (**8 total**).

4 bars	FORWARD 3 AND BACK: First gent advances and retires with the two ladies (**8 total**).

4 bars — FORWARD AGAIN TO BALANCE CIRCLE: First gent and ladies advance to meet the second gent, all joining hands in a circle (4) to balance forward touch and back touch (**8 total**).

4 bars — FOUR HANDS HALF AROUND: These four dancers turn their circle CW halfway around to the left, and retire to the opposite couple's position (**8 total**).

4 bars — HALF RIGHT AND LEFT: Couples Half Right and Left back to place (**8 total**).

Sides repeat above figure.

Figure 5 (32 bars and 8-bar finale)

16-count intro.

8 bars — ALL PROMENADE: All four couples promenade CCW once around the set back to original places (**16 total**).[10]

8 bars — BALANCE/HALF RIGHT AND LEFT: Head couples forward 4 and back 4, then walk forward, passing through each other with the ladies in the middle, touching R. hands with opposite as they pass to the opposite side. Head gents turn the ladies with L. hands so partners are facing (**16 total**).

8 bars — CHASSEZ/HALF RIGHT AND LEFT BACK: Head couple partners face each other and Chassez 4 to their right, away from each other (ladies into the middle and gents to the outside) and back together 4. Head couples face in to Half Right and Left back to original positions (8) (**16 total**).

8 bars — HEAD COUPLES CHASSEZ ACROSS AND BACK: Head couples face partners to take crossed hands (R. on top) and slide across the set, with

gents back-to-back turning CCW (8) to return (**16 total**).

Sides repeat above figure.

Finale (8 bars)

4 bars — ALL CHASSEZ: All couples face and Chassez to the right four steps away from each other, ladies into the center and gents away from the set, and return (**8 total**).

4 bars — TWO-HAND TURN AND SALUTE: All Two-Hand Turn their partners once CW (4) and end with a salute (bow and curtsy) to each other (**8 total**). Each gent then offers his arm to his partner, to lead her off the floor.

SOURCES: *Dick's Quadrille Call-Book* (New York: Dick & Fitzgerald, Publishers, 1878), 30–34; Elias Howe, *American Dancing Master and Ballroom Prompter* (Boston: Miles & Dillingham Printers, 1866), 10; Edward Ferrero, *The Art of Dancing* (New York: self-published, 1859), 122–26; Thomas Hillgrove, *A Complete Practical Guide to the Art of Dancing* (New York: Dick & Fitzgerald, 1867), 65.

Notes for Archival Dances

1. S. Foster Damon, "The History of Square Dancing," *American Antiquarian Society* vol. 62, no. 1, 86.

2. Brigham Young, as quoted in Richard Burton, *The City of the Saints: Among the Mormons and across the Rocky Mountains to California* (New York: Harper and Brothers, 1862).

3. Marlbrouk performed by the Missouri History Museum by Dance Discovery. Recorded December 12, 2010. Youtube video; www.youtube.com/watch?v=JFB2El3hxL8.

4. Brigham Young, quoted in Richard Burton, *The City of the Saints: Among the Mormons and across the Rocky Mountains to California* (New York: Harper and Brothers, 1862), 230–31.

5. H. P. Larsen, *Pioneer Songs* (Salt Lake City: Daughters of Utah Pioneers, 1932), 276.

6. The sheet music for this dance is not included in this book. See *The New Caledonian Quadrille* (Boston: Oliver Ditson and Co., 1859). Available at the University of North Carolina at Chapel Hill Library. See also dc.lib.unc.edu/cdm/ref/collection /sheetmusic/id/30812.

7. Thomas Hillgrove, *A Complete Practical Guide to the Art of Dancing* (New York: Dick & Fitzgerald, 1867), 61–62.

8. Aunt Carrie, *Popular Pastimes for Field and Fireside, or Amusements for Young and Old* (Springfield: Milton Bradley & Co., 167), 141.

9. The sheet music for this dance is not included in this book. See *The Mormons: Quadrille*, Charles Coote Jr. (London: Hopwood and Crew, 1860). Available at the University of Utah J. Willard Marriot Library, the Brigham Young University Harold B. Lee Library, and the University of California–Santa Barbara Library.

10. All Circle Left (8) and Right (8) may be substituted for All Promenade (16).

Appendix A

FIDDLING AND DANCING UNTO THE LORD

Mark Jardine

Religion and art, music and dance have always enjoyed a rather tenuous relationship. Early American Christian views on music and its place in religion varied greatly. Some Christian religions viewed music in their devotions and services—even hymn singing—as sacrilegious. Others felt music to be the highest form of praise for the Lord. As early American Christian churches developed, a major question was, "What part, if any, does music play in the religious community and experience?" The Church of Jesus Christ of Latter-day Saints (LDS) was not exempt from this question.[1]

After the Church was first organized in 1830, this musical question was resolved early on in their history when Joseph Smith Jr., prophet and founder of the Church, received a revelation from God that Joseph's wife Emma should compile a book of religious hymns from the Christian tradition for the edifying of the Saints (see D&C 25:11–12). This ultimately led to the compilation and publication of "A Collection of Sacred Hymns for the Church of Jesus Christ of Latter-day Saints"

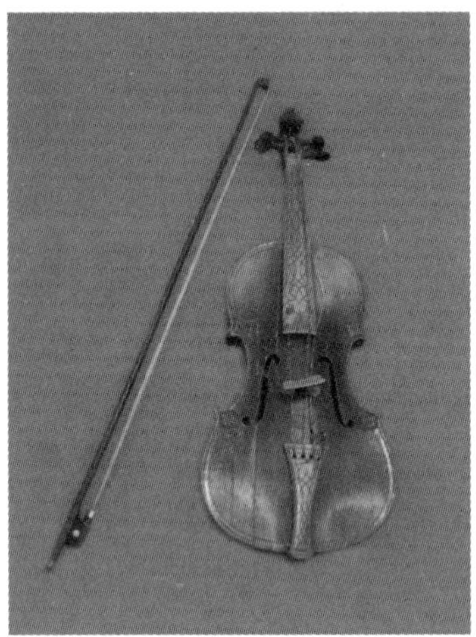

William Pitt, pioneer of 1847 and well-known band leader, brought this violin across the plains which he played left-handed. Photo courtesy of the Daughters of Utah Pioneers' Salt Lake City Pioneer Memorial Museum.

(1835). Hymn singing had become accepted and had become an important part of Mormon devotion and praise for the Lord.

Instrumental church music, and especially secular music, was a different question. In this period of American Christian history, the fiddle was often viewed as the instrument of the devil. Fiddle music and dancing were seen as being associated with taverns, drinking, and general debauchery. Brigham Young, the second LDS prophet, when recalling his youth, stated, "I never heard the enchanting tones of the violin until I was eleven years of age, and then I thought I was on the highway to hell, if I suffered myself to linger and listen to it."[2] Early American Christian evangelists (LDS included) prided themselves in converting fiddlers and dancers, convincing them to destroy their instruments, and thereby "saving their souls." Levi Hancock, an early prominent Mormon, and his brothers were convinced to destroy their fiddles before they could join the Church.[3] Most of the leadership and members of the Church had grown up having these negative feelings regarding fiddling and dancing distilled upon them.

"Church records confirm that a year and a half after the dedication of the Kirtland Temple (the first LDS temple, built in Kirtland, Ohio: Dedicated March 27, 1836), the local high priests of the Church disfellowshipped twenty-two members who had attended a local dance in the community."[4]

As history has shown, fiddling and dancing prevailed!

As a distinct Mormon community grew and thrived, the members began to re-evaluate their stance on fiddling and dancing. In their new context, fiddling and dancing were no longer seen as being connected to taverns, alcohol consumption, and debauchery, but became more a part of the social fabric of their community.

As a religious community, the people saw all their endeavors, done in the right spirit, as giving praise to the Lord. Their daily lives and their religious beliefs were inseparable.

Brigham Young later reversed his previous view on the evils of the fiddle and stated, "Every decent fiddler will go into a decent kingdom" (in the after-life).[5] As both a Mormon and "a decent fiddler," I take great comfort, joy, and humor from this statement.

William Clayton, a musician in the early Church, recorded in his journal a dance held in the Nauvoo Temple (the second LDS temple, built in Nauvoo, Illinois). Brigham Young described the musicians (a flute player and fiddle player) playing "The Fisher's Hornpipe," as a common nineteenth-century dance tune while the group danced a "French Four." Clayton went on to describe that after the dance, "Brigham Young called attention of the whole community, and gave them a message of this import, viz; that this Temple was a Holy place, and 'when we danced, we danced unto the Lord.'"[6]

As the saints in Nauvoo grew as a community, outsiders persecuted them for their beliefs more and more. The decision was made for the members to "move out West." There, they would eventually settle the Salt Lake Valley. This migration

This large, square grand piano was brought to Utah in 1862. Its legs were removed in order for the body to fit flat in a covered wagon. This heavy instrument made it to Wyoming, but had to be left there since it was slowing down the speed of the wagon company. It was wrapped in buffalo robes, with the fur side to the piano, and was buried. Its owner returned a year later to retrieve it. This happened to a number of these treasured instruments.

Photo courtesy of the Daughters of Utah Pioneers' Salt Lake City Pioneer Memorial Museum

caused significant hardships and suffering. Many of the pioneers died en route to Salt Lake. Brigham Young recognized the importance of keeping up the spirits of the pioneers in their arduous journey. "He encouraged nightly singing and dancing along the trail as the Mormons traveled west and even sometimes had the snow cleared away so the people could dance, keep their spirits up, and stay warm."[7] In this pioneer culture, dance had become one of the primary forms of entertainment, socialization, encouragement, and spiritual expression.

Mormons have always been an active proselytizing church. Once settled in Utah, the call went out for member converts to flock to "Zion" (the Salt Lake Valley). Converts from America, England, Ireland, Wales, the Isle of Man, and Scandinavia came to Utah. Each group brought with them their own song and dance traditions from their native countries. Different from most "melting pot" cultures, where the Irish, German, and so on would settle within their own communities, Mormons were different. Their glue was not their native cultures (although those cultures remained important to them), but rather the gospel and the doctrine of their Church.

Early Utah dance music included American, Scottish, Irish, Welsh, and Scandinavian dance tunes, which the bands blended for the common good of the community. Records show that the different styles of musicians played together in the same bands. It was not uncommon to see the band made up of a musician playing "violin" and another playing "the fiddle." This is yet another indication of the Saints' willingness to blend styles and types of music in praise of the Lord.

Early typical Utah dance band instrumentation included the fiddle, the organ, the accordion, concertina, flute, cello, and bass. Later, when the railroad came, guitars, mandolins, and banjos began to appear. During the breaks, or breathers between dances, "party pieces" were often performed. Programs document that Scottish Reels, humorous songs, and demonstrations of English Morris dancing or step dancing were performed. The musical flavor of these dances seems more akin to the current traditions of contra dancing than what we think of as American square dancing.

Brigham Young was eager to further colonize and establish communities throughout the west. He sent pioneers to settle parts of Utah, Nevada, Idaho, and Arizona.

Once again, with the idea of boosting the pioneers' spirits, musicians were an integral part of the dance parties. The suggestion was made to form choirs, have dances, put on plays, and so on. A good example of this can be found in the book, *History of Iron County Mission: Parowan, UT.*

Parowan was the "mother settlement" of Southern Utah. One of the companies sent to settle Parowan was Thomas Durham, a famous early Utah musician. "As Parowan was established, story has it that one night a mass meeting was held to decide what was the best way to light the church. Someone suggested buying a beautiful chandelier to hold the oil lamps. One of the brethren, unclear on what a chandelier was, rose to his feet and said, "'What's the use buying a thing like that when no one but brother Durham can play it.'"[8]

The same book on the history of Parowan, Utah, describes a typical dance held in 1851 at the Log Counsel House in Parowan.

As this was to be a rather swell affair, extra exertion was made to obtain the best of music, regardless of expense, and so two fiddlers were engaged instead of one, the usual number. Each gentleman was expected to bring two candles to pay for their ticket; those not burned were to go to the musicians for their pay. This was no small matter as candles were very scarce, and were kept in reserve for cases of sickness or other extra occasions.

> This wise arrangement as to the candles promised a brilliant room, but unfortunately when the time arrived to light up, it was found no one had brought a candlestick. . . . The committee . . . had entirely forgotten his necessary appendage to a candle. Some took their jack knives and stuck a blade into a log, and this, when partly closed, would hold a candle very well. Others rushed home and brought large potatoes or turnips which were transformed quickly into candlesticks by slicing off the bottom for a base and by making a hole in the top to hold the candle.

Then we come to the dance!

> The musicians were seated at one end of the room upon a table. The younger part of the company showed unmistakable signs of impatience until the Bishop in humble prayer asks the blessings of God upon the evening's enjoyment. . . . Then the floor manger cries, "Numbers one to twelve" and all those holding those tickets rush for their partners. The

> numbers by the way were drawn lottery fashion from a hat passed around at the commencement.[9]

The dance was on.

People came from miles around for the dances, and these events often lasted for a few days. Picnics were brought, and kids were often allowed to sleep along the walls as the dance progressed, often going all night. The dance was the primary social event.

As Utah communities grew and more people settled in who were not of the Mormon faith, the dances became less and less under the auspices of the Church. The music and dance prevailed once again. It was no longer seen as a specifically Mormon event with overtones of their beliefs, but a general place for people to socialize. The dynamics of the dance had changed. These dynamics are best described in the lyrics of the traditional cowboy song, "The Mormon Cowboy":[10]

1) I am a Mormon cowboy / Utah is my home
Tucson, Arizona / is the first place I did roam.
And then unto El Capitan / A place you all know well
To describe that brushy country / no mortal tongue can tell.

2) I was at the old post office / when a maid came riding down
She rode a bronco pony / and soon was on the ground.
She gave to each and everyone / an invitation grand
She invited us to a grand ball / at the old El Capitan

3) We all went to the dance that night / at the schoolhouse by the road
Some folks come from Drippin' Springs / and many came from Globe
The music they brought with them / I never shall forget
'Twas a colored man with his guitar / I can hear him playin' yet.

4) There were many married women there / and single gals too;
I soon became acquainted / with all except a few.
The cowboys in their high heeled boots / were leading the Grand March.
While the city dudes soon followed / with their collars stiff with starch.

5) After dancing two or three sets / I went outside to cool,
But every bush that I passed by / was loaded with white mule
They finally fed us supper / it was a quarter past one
I heard a fight had broken out / each cowboy grabbed his gun.

6) Up stepped a little cowpuncher / his eyes were flashing fire,
He said he was a ramrod / at a ranch called 'Bar F Bar'
I started for my pony / the guns were flashing fast
I could hear a cowboy shouting / they broke it up at last.

7) So I bid farewell to my new made friends / and a place called El Capitan
The fairest face I ever saw / was in that wild and happy band.
I jumped into my saddle / and started out for home
I made up my mind right there and then / I never more would roam.

Music and dance historically have persisted regardless of the religious or political environment. As the religious context of Utah dance music began to melt away, fiddling and dancing continued to be the primary source of entertainment, joy, and expression as evidenced by the number of square dances, contra dances, Irish and Scottish dances, and other nationalities' dances present in Mormon country today: May we all continue to sing, play, and dance our praises to life!

Notes

1. Michael Hicks, *Mormonism and Music* (Urbana and Chicago: University of Illinois Press 1989), ch. 1.

2. Ibid., 5.

3. Ibid., 79.

4. Ibid., 74–75.

5. Ibid., 79.

6. George W. Smith, ed. *An Intimate Chronicle: the Journals of William Clayton* (Salt Lake City: Signature Books, 1995), 247.

7. Hicks, *Mormonism and Music.*

8. Mrs. Luella Adams Dalton, "An Old Time Dancing Party," *History of Iron County Mission; Parowan, Utah* (Parowan: No publisher or date noted), 325, 277.

9. Ibid., 548.

10. *Old-Time Cowboy Songs*, dir. and ed. Hal Cannon (Layton: Gibbs Smith, 1998), book; and (Newton: Shanachie Records, 1985), cassette.

Appendix B

MORMON PIONEER ERA CLOTHING FOR THE DANCE

Jaynanne Meads

There are five overriding factors that govern clothing worn during the pioneer period. Two of the most obvious considerations are gender and age. Other significant dynamics include economic status and the distance from major trade centers, which determined availability and choice of materials. All of these principles function under the umbrella of prevailing contemporary culture, which includes social mores and fashion trends.

In regard to the aspects of gender and age a few general notes are of interest, which we will address later in the chapter.

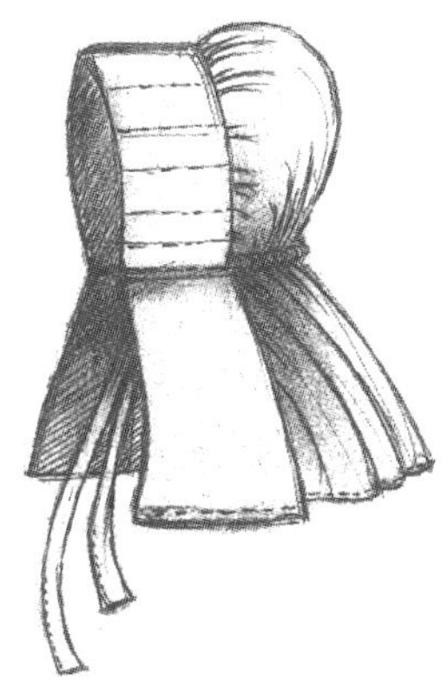

As in all cultures, household financial resources, skills of production, and the availability of materials played significant roles in determining what exactly people wore. A kind of continuum existed where the richest people in

Salt Lake wore clothing very similar to those in other metropolitan areas of the time. But in general, the farther from Salt Lake and its economic development and skilled labor force one moved, the farther down the clothing continuum one expected to descend. A simple example might be that in Salt Lake City, where there were several men's tailors, a man might wear a tailcoat to a formal occasion. Fifty miles away in Provo, a man might wear a frock coat, which was serviceable for a variety of occasions. Farther away still a man's best coat may have been a sack coat because his wife made it. Regardless of finances or other factors, a people choose to wear their best clothes, whatever they were, to a formal, public occasion.

Fashion Versus Homespun

Mormons were at least as influenced by current fashions as other groups of settlers. It is reported that ladies magazines that noted the most current fashions in Paris, New York, and London were carried to the fledgling community on the first wagon train carrying supplies from the east. Even though Brigham Young and Heber C. Kimball preached from the pulpit about self-sufficiency and the use of homespun clothes and homemade straw bonnets, their wives and children followed contemporary fashion trends and often dressed in embellished silk gowns. Women of the territory took note and followed their example when possible. The handmade nature of clothing of the period, the distance from fashion centers, and other obstacles of settling a new territory made the acquisition of many and varied items of clothing a slow process. It might take several years for a "new" style to become fashionable in Deseret.

Women's Clothing Essentials to Create the Pioneer Period Silhouette

Chemise and Drawers

With these factors in mind, we can explore the fashion continuum in greater detail, outlining standard silhouettes and fabrics with common variations and details. Women wore a cotton or linen chemise next to the skin on the top of the body. These were not seen, and the drawstring neckline of the eighteenth century had been replaced with a smooth fitted neckline or yoke. The narrow, turned hem reached to about the knees. Under the chemise was a pair of drawers, which consisted of two legs that were each often gathered to a yoke or waistband. The legs were not joined in the crotch area and back to facilitate toileting. The hems of the drawer legs were decorated with crocheted lace, tucks or ribbon. Straight legs appear to have been more common than legs gathered into a band at the knee. Elastic was not used in underclothing at this time.

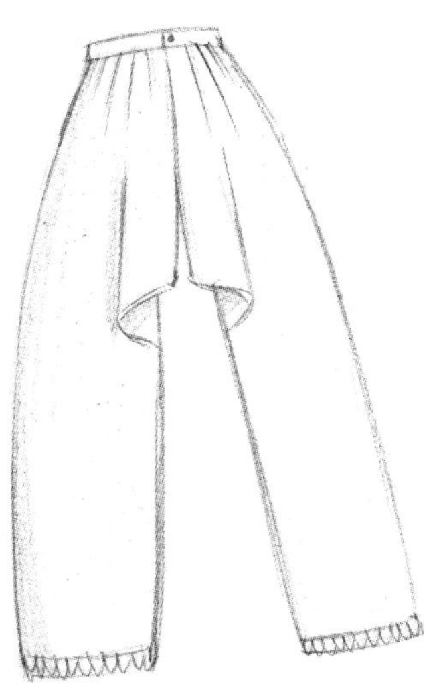

Stays or Corset

Over the chemise and drawers, a woman wore either stays (an un-boned supportive bodice) or a corset, the purposes of which were to create a fashionable silhouette, support the breasts, and smooth the figure. Stays and corsets were often made of "drab" cotton or linen coutil, a strong twill-woven fabric, something like lightweight denim that did not stretch. Period corsets were usually reinforced with whalebone, but modern reproductions use spring steel "bones." Eyelets were hand sewn over brass rings for strength and were placed at the center back.

Separating busks (the rigid portion in the center front of the corset with hooks and eyes) appeared in the mid-1850s and were common thereafter, making getting into a corset by oneself much easier. Corsets and stays of the 1840s and 1850s often had shoulder straps. These straps gradually disappeared and were gone by the 1860s. Reproduction corsets should be made for each individual according to their own body symmetry to avoid discomfort. Tight lacing should be avoided when dancing, since a tightly laced corset can diminish lung capacity by up to 40 percent.

Petticoats

Next, over the chemise and drawers, petticoats were added. In the 1840s a number of petticoats were worn to fill out the skirts to the desired width. Some historians estimate the number of petticoats to be between five and seven. Before the invention of the hoop skirt, corded petticoats were required. Several horizontal rows of cording were inserted from the hem to the knees to make the skirts stand out and to avoid the skirts wadding up between the legs. After the advent of the cage, crinoline petticoat numbers decreased to about three—one under the hoop for modesty, should the hoop blow in the wind, and two over the hoop to protect the dress skirt from the metal hoop. Petticoats were gathered or pleated to a waistband or a shaped yoke which closed with a fabric, thread, or a flat mother of pearl or bone button. Some petticoats had a drawstring casing at the top to allow for the changing female figure. The hem of the petticoat could be embroidered, tucked, ruffled, or plain according to the taste and skill of the woman. Quilted petticoats had a quilted panel that reached from the hem to mid-thigh and had

the advantages of being warmer and stiffer. Knitted wool petticoats were also common in the colder months of the year. Economy suggested that dress skirts were often repurposed as petticoats when the bodices wore out. Best petticoats were often white, heavily starched embroidered linen or cotton. Silk taffeta petticoats were also popular. Crinoline, a stiff fabric of horsehair and linen, was also used in petticoats as a hem stiffener and also as complete petticoats. There was a craze for red woolen petticoats embroidered in black silk in the 1860s. Patterns for such embroidery are readily available in Godey's Ladies' Magazine.

Corset Cover

You might think we are done with underwear, but there is one more item of clothing—a corset cover. During the 1840s, fabric flaps on the chemise folded over the corset at front and back neckline and on the shoulders to hold the straps in place. These flaps protected the dress from rubbing on the corset bones and prevented the consequent wear. Sometime during the 1850s these flaps fell out of fashion and a new garment, the "underbody" or corset cover, took their place. A corset cover was worn between the corset and the dress to prevent the corset from wearing out the dress. During the 1850s and 1860s these corset covers closely resembled the cut of the dress under which they were worn and terminated in a waistband or had a small peplum-type skirt below the waist and buttoned up the front or back. The corset covers usually had short sleeves, either plain straight ones or small puffed sleeves with a band. Corset covers were usually of white cotton or linen.

Women's Pioneer Period Dresses

Dresses are analyzed by looking at the basic silhouette and at the popularity of various necklines, waist treatments, sleeves, and decorations. The general silhouette is considered an hourglass shape, with a small waist and voluminous skirts and snug-fitting bodices. Most bodice backs of the time were cut with what we would term princess lines, the seam running from no more than two inches from the center back at the waist in a curve across the shoulder blades to the armholes. Armholes were elliptical and the shoulder line fell down the arm about three or four inches. The shoulder seam was rotated toward the back at the sleeve side two to three inches. These general characteristics continue throughout the mid-nineteenth century and apply today as well as eveningwear.

1840s

In addition to the above-mentioned qualities, dresses of the 1840s had their own peculiar feel. They had a linear, droopy look. Some of the elements that contribute to the look are "V" necklines, long tight sleeves or slightly belled ones, slightly elongated waistlines with a point in front and sometimes in back, vertical folds of fabric or pleats on the bodice front, and applied vertical trims or flanges on the bodice. Skirts reached to the floor, leaving only enough clearance to not trip on one's skirt. For formal occasions the neckline broadened to almost fall from the shoulders. Often a wide collar, called a bertha, was attached to the neckline and fell over the arms. Other times gathered or pleated fabric emphasized the breast area. Younger ladies wore short, puffed, or straight sleeves. Older

women might continue to wear full-length sleeves, even for formal occasions. A garment peculiar to the 1840s is a pelerine made of the same fabric as the dress. A pelerine was a narrow, cape-like garment, which hung down in the front and back to about waist level but left the arms free. Pelerines were used to cover the lower neckline of an afternoon dress to make it suitable for daywear or merely to change the look of a dress.

1850s

Dresses of the 1850s create a wide, horizontal look with full, bell-shaped skirts with horizontal lines and shoulder details. Skirts were pleated or gauged to the bodice at the natural waistline. Although dresses were usually made in one piece at this time, if the skirt was attached to a waistband, it gave the opportunity for creating two bodices to be worn with the same skirt, one for evening wear with a low neckline and short sleeves, and another for day wear with a jewel neckline and long sleeves. Common characteristics of the 1850s are skirts with tiered layers of gathered flounces attached to an underskirt and pagoda sleeves, a wide bell-shaped sleeve that required the use of white cotton or linen under sleeves.

Other popular sleeves of the day are coat sleeves cut in a "C" shape (sometimes called a banana sleeve); bagpipe sleeves with a large bulge at the elbow; and, for work dresses, a bishop's sleeve, gathered into a cuff at the wrist. Necklines for daywear were near the throat, where a white collar was usually attached. These collars were made of linen or cotton and could be embellished with white embroidery or lace. Embroidery or lace patterns for sets of under sleeves and matching collars were often advertised in ladies'

magazines of the day. An interesting note from period publications suggested that crocheted lace collars were appropriate for wearing at home but were not suitable for visiting or other activities outside the home. A general lack of period crochet patterns for collars and under sleeves would also suggest this was a general view. One supposes that this opinion was held because of the connection crocheted lace had to the decoration of underwear of the period, or may, in fact, reflect the derisive view of the Irish, who were famous for their crocheted laces. Necklines for evening continued to be wide and nearly off the shoulder. Bertha collars continued to be worn, although fabric gathered across the chest had disappeared. Short, puffed sleeves were very popular for evening.

1860s

By the 1860s, railroad travel had become more common and had an effect on women's clothing, particularly their skirts. Wide bell-shaped hoop skirts became less round and were squished into an ellipse to accommodate narrow aisles and the close quarter of train travel. During the 1840s and 50s, skirts had been sewn from rectangular lengths of fabric of the desired length. In the 1860s these rectangular panels were shaped into trapezoids. This had the effect of narrowing the skirt near the waist and creating a much more streamlined appearance. The skirt in front, over the tummy, began to flatten out and much of the fullness of the skirt moved to the back. Skirts often touched the ground in back with a small sweep in preparation for the bustle, which appeared in the 1870s. During the 1860s young girls and teenagers began to wear skirts and

bodices of different fabrics with a short bolero or Zouave jacket. Older women eschewed the style.

Women's Accessories

Women's accessories at formal occasions included gloves, jewelry, hair ornaments, and fans. If a woman was wearing short sleeves, full-length kid gloves were preferred. Pendant earrings in a teardrop shape were popular during the mid-century and were often worn with a matching necklace. If a woman had no jewels she was free to wear a small nosegay of flowers between the breasts or at the waist. Small silver vases that pinned to the dress were made for the purpose. Fans were a practical concern for dances in the days before central air-conditioning and were made of paper, silk, or lace. Hair ornaments were often constructed on a circlet of buckram and were covered in silk or velvet. Loops of ribbon, artificial flowers, or feathers were added for decoration. During the 1840s, just as with dresses, the general feeling was droopy, and flowers, feathers, and ribbons cascaded downward on either side of the face. In the 1850s, the idea was to add width to the face to create another horizontal line, so decorations were at the sides of the head. By the 1860s, decorations had moved to include the back of the head, much as skirts had moved to the back.

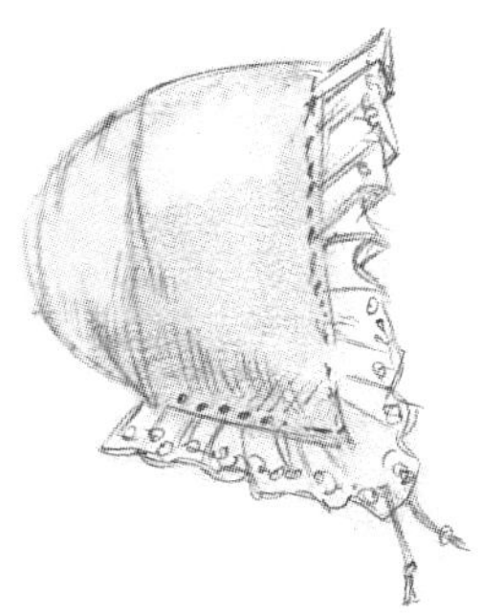

Shoes for Dancing

For dancing in the 1840s flat slippers were preferred. They could be made of satin or soft leather and have rounded or square toes. Ribbons crisscrossed the instep and tied at the ankle, much like modern ballet toe shoes. By the 1850s, cloth booties had become popular as dance shoes. They were often made of cloth to match the gown, with leather toe and heel caps and laced off the side of the shoe. The 1860s dance shoes were pump-like with short, curvy French heels.

Pioneer Period Men's Clothing

Shirts

Men's fashions of the time do not manifest as much change in comparison to women's fashions. Men's underwear was considerably less restrictive. They wore cotton or linen shirts and drawers. Shirts were primarily constructed of rectangles and squares until some shaping began in the body to give a smother fit to the vest or waistcoat, which was worn over it in the 1860s. A collar was attached at the neckline and had a center front placket opening that might close with cloth, thread, or mother of pearl or bone buttons. The button that closed the collar was obligatory, but the other buttons might be dispensed with depending on economic and social factors. Shirts were most commonly made of white cotton with center front placket openings. Dressier shirts often had a "bosom"—an inset piece of fabric surrounding the opening with decorative pleats or ruffles. Detachable bosoms were also available. The shirt collar might have been detachable, being buttoned at the back of the neck. Collars were stiffly starched and worn turned up, appearing above the tie or cravat, but by the mid-1850s were less stiff and were turned down over the tie. Work shirts of the 1840s and 50s were more amply cut and were made of woven stripes, check, or plain colors and of either cotton or wool.

Neckties

The most popular necktie of the 1840s was made of soft fabric and was tied in a horizontal knot. Both light and dark colored silks were used. Older gentlemen or those with a military background may have opted for a stock—a silk- or satin-covered wired frame that buckled in back. A narrow black "string" tie was also worn. By the 1850s, the style of tying the tie had changed to a silk square, which was folded in from two opposing sides to create a rather stiff, horizontal half bow with the ends sticking out to one side. Black was common for daywear, and checks or plaids appealed to younger, more fashionable men. Narrow black ties and soft silk bows continue to be worn well into the 1860s.

Trousers

Fall front trousers were most used by the working class and made of washable materials such as heavy cotton, linen, or wool. They were adjustable at the back with a strap or a drawstring. Trousers of this sort were of neutral colors or sometimes of blue stripe or small checked patterns. However, button fly trousers were in general use for dress as well as business situations. Black wool was the overall favorite color for dress in the 1840s and 50s. Pant legs were rather narrower in the 1840s, gradually growing wider in the early 50s. Trousers were not creased as they are today, and appeared quite round. Among the younger crowd, the 1850s brought a fad for checked and plaid pants and light-colored cotton or linen trousers in the summer months.

Vests

Double-breasted vests usually had shawl collars. Single-breasted vests could have notched or shawl collars. Less common were single-breasted vests without a collar at all. Vests had two tabs applied to the back near the waist with three or four pairs of hand-sewn eyelets, which were laced to the appropriate tightness to define the waist. During the 1850s, black double-breasted vests that matched the coat were considered business dress. In the summer, these were swapped out for tan or white colored cotton or linen vests. Patterned silk vests were most popular for eveningwear. There was also a fad for checks and plaid vests.

Coats

Men's coats were of three major types—tailcoat, now only for the most formal of occasions; frock coat, a snug-fitting body with a rather full skirt and tight sleeves; and newer "saque" or sack coat, which resembled a limp modern suit coat. During the 1840s and early 1850s, the coats had quite narrow sleeves with a slight puff set into a lowered armhole. In the 1850s the armhole became higher and sleeves were cut wider.

Hats

The wearing of a hat was an essential part of getting dressed for every man. Poor indeed was the man without one. Hats for men were usually in fur felt or silk top hat styles, fabric caps being left to young men. For business, hard black derby hats were popular. For dress, silk top hats were required. Fur felt hats in black, brown, tan, or cream were shaped in various styles and often modified by the wearer.

Boots and Shoes

Men wore black, short, pull-on boots with square toes and low, wide heels. Low oxford-type shoes with square toes were also popular. For dancing and formal occasions, men wore black, lightweight slip-on pumps, which might have tied over the instep with a ribbon.

Pioneer Children's Clothing

Children usually wore clothing resembling their parents, with the exception of young boys, who often wore skirted tunics over short trousers until the age of about three or four. Short pants were often worn until the approximate age of twelve. Long pants were practical in rural areas and were also worn by young boys. The length of girls' skirts was determined by their age. . . . Toddler skirts started just below the knee and were lengthened a couple of inches periodically as the girl aged, until the skirts reached the top of her boots at around age sixteen. Skirts of mature women brushed the instep of the foot in front and may have touched the ground in the back.

Sources

1. Laughing Moon Mercantile: Mid-nineteenth-century pioneer period clothing patterns; www.lafnmoon.com.

2. Past Patterns: Saundra Ros Altman's Past Patterns, the Historical Pattern Company Dedicated to Accuracy 1850s–1860s Patterns; www.pastpatterns.com/1850.html.

3. Truly Victorian Sewing Patterns: www.trulyvictorian.net.

4. Fig Leaf Patterns and Patterns Only: www.figleafpatterns .com/gallery.html (some pioneer period children's patterns).

5. Elizabeth Stewart Clark: The Sewing Academy; www .thesewingacademy.com/shop (some pioneer period children's patterns).

6. Clothing The Saints: Mormon Pioneer period clothing and Mormon Trek modifications; www.clothingthesaints.com.

Jaynanne Meads is a costume specialist for the Theater Department at Brigham Young University.

Glossary

ABBREVIATIONS

Clockwise (CW): The rotation direction of an individual, couple, group, or general circle, according to the movement of the hands of a clock if it were placed flatly face up on the floor.

Counter-Clockwise (CCW): The opposite of CCW rotation.

Line of Dance (LOD): The direction dancers are facing or progressing in a circle moving CCW around the room.

Reverse Line of Dance (RLOD): The opposite of CCW rotation.

R. and L.: Right and Left.

(8), (16), (24) etc.: The number of counts, or steps, in a previous figure.

TERMINOLOGY

Active Couples: The couples who start the dance. In **contra dancing**, it would be the top couple plus, in duple minor, every other couple below (1-3-5, etc.) or in triple minor, top couple and every third couple (1-4-7-10-13, etc.). In some longways set dances, the top couple only is active. In **quadrilles**, the head couples (1 and 2) are active first to perform the figure. Then the sides (3 and 4) become active to repeat the same figure.

Allemande: A Right- or Left-Hand Turn once around, usually with a corner or a partner.

Balance: An 8-count balance is walking forward 4 and back 4. "**Advance and Retire**" is an English country dance term also used for an 8-count balance. A 4-count balance can be a "side, touch, side, touch," "forward touch, back touch," "two steps forward and two steps back," or "pas de basque" Scottish style, as described in Caledonian Quadrille. Old Dan Tucker features the 4-count step-swing, step-swing balance.

The "Pigeon Wing," a 4-count show-off balance, is stepping on the R. foot and swinging the left across high in front to shake or "twizzle" the L. foot side-to-side, while hopping on the right, then repeating this on the left side. It took some strength and skill to "cut a pigeon wing," which was a specialty of Brigham Young who loved "muscular" fancy footwork.

Ballroom Position: Also referred to as "closed ballroom position." Partners are facing and hold each other as follows: the palm of the gent's R. hand is on the small of the lady's back. The lady's L. hand rests on the gent's R. shoulder. The gent is holding the lady's R. hand in his L. This was a scandalous hold for round dances such as the waltz and polka, which were first frowned upon, then prohibited by Mormon clergy in the latter part of the nineteenth century.

Bottom of the set: The end of a longways set furthest from the band and caller.

Bow: The formal nineteenth-century bow is executed in four counts. On count one, the gent takes a small step to the side with the R. foot. Count two, he closes the L. foot to the right. Count three, he bends slightly forward with the upper body. Count four, he straightens.

Cast Around: The figure after the active couples in a longways set return from going down the center. They separate and walk down behind and around the inactive, or #2 couple, taking their place while #2 couple moved up the set into #1's place.

Cast off down the set: In a contra, or longways set, the top couple, or active couples, turn away from each other to walk down the outside of the longways set.

Change: A term in a cotillion that means once through a specific figure.

Chassez, Chasse, Sashay: A sliding step to the side, a sped-up side-close step.

Circle: A single circle holding hands, usually CW and returning CCW. It is also referred to as hands 3, hands 4, hands 6, or hands, designating how many couples are in a circle.

Contra dance: Is derived from the English term "country dance." It consists of a longways set of two parallel lines of partners facing across. Active couples, in the smaller (minor) groups of two or three, progress down to the bottom of the set, while inactive couples progress up to the top of the set where they become active. Actives who reach the bottom of the set become inactive.

Corner: The person on the left for the gents and on the right for the ladies in a circle or quadrille.

Cotillion: The forerunner of the quadrille. Both the cotillion and the quadrille consisted of four couples in a square formation of French origin. The cotillion was popular in the late 1700s and early 1800s. It was associated with peasantry and was quite boisterous and energetic, with fancy footwork and show-off steps danced to traditional folk tunes. The structure was that of changes (different figures or formations), followed by a set chorus figure. The word "cotillion" is a French term referring to a peasant girl's petticoat. The word "cotillion" was often used interchangeably with "quadrille," especially in America. The term "cotillion" was also used for a dance party and a square set of four couples.

During the latter half of the nineteenth century, a dancing game called "Cotillion," or "The German," became popular. It consisted of intricate group patterns with changing partners, which were called or led by a conductor with an encyclopedic knowledge of hundreds of games and patterns. These dancing games were often danced with waltz, polka, and mazurka steps.

Cross Over: Dancers change places across the contra set by walking forward, pivoting CCW face-to-face in the center of the set, and backing up to original side, as in Miss McCleod's Reel and French Four

Curtsy (or courtesy): The formal nineteenth-century curtsy, like the bow, is executed in four counts. Count one, the lady takes a small step to the side with her R. foot. Count two, she steps behind with her L. foot. Count three, she bends both knees placing her weight on the back L. foot and lifting the heel of the R. foot. Count four, she brings the back L. foot up to the R. foot.

Cut-a-Sha: A quadrille term equivalent to "rights and lefts" in English country dance, or "square through" in Western square dancing. Two couples, heads or sides, walk forward to execute a Mini-Grand Right and Left, or chain, as follows: Take opposite by the R. hand, pulling by to turn a quarter and take partner by the L., turn a quarter and take opposite by the R. hand to turn a quarter and take partner by the L. hand.

Dos-a-Dos: Facing partners walk toward each other passing R. shoulders, slide back to back and back up, passing L. shoulders, to place without turning. It is known as "back to back" in English country dance and translated the same in French.

Down the Center and Back: In a contra or longways set, this is a 16-count figure where active couples step into the center of the longways set, taking inside hands to walk down the set about 6 steps, then turn toward each other, or as a couple, to walk back up the set.

Duple Minor: A longways set dance divided into two couple sections, active and inactive, working together to perform the dance figure.

Figure: A set sequence of dance moves in a quadrille. Quadrilles typically have four or five figures, with a brief break in between. Each figure has different music.

Grand Chain (Grand Right and Left): Partners face each other, take R. hands, pull by to take left with the next, repeating this around the quadrille set. Ladies are moving CW and gents CCW. Partners meet each other halfway around the set and may take a promenade position to return to place CCW, or continue around the set until they meet again at home position. As Western square dancing evolved, this became a "Grand Right and Left."

Hands Across: A four-person star figure where a dancer holds the hand of the person directly across from them in the star. Right-hand stars turn CW and Left-Hand Stars turn CCW. A "Moulinet" (whirl around) is a French term that was often used for this figure.

Head Couples: In a quadrille, this refers to couples 1 and 2, who are the first to dance a figure. Couple #1 is at the top of the quadrille with their backs to the caller and music.

Ladies Chain: In a **quadrille,** the head (or side) two ladies cross, giving R. hands as they pass, and L. hands to the opposite gent. The two gents turn the opposite lady around by leading her with L. hand around to face back into the set. (This is the same as a courtesy turn, only omitting the gent's hand on the ladies back.) The two ladies return to their partners in the same fashion. In a **contra dance** this same figure is danced across the set.

Longways Set: Two lines of dancers facing their partner across the set. This can refer to a contra dance formation or a set with an earlier figure having the top couple active only, as in the Virginia Reel.

Minor: A grouping of dancers in contra dances. (i.e. two couples working together to dance the figure [in a duple minor] or three couples working together to dance the figure [in a triple minor].)

Pas Marchez: French terminology for "walking step," danced in an elegantly flowing manner as in nineteenth-century quadrilles.

Polka: A very vigorous dance step performed as "hop step-close-step" in an uneven (dotted) 2/4 rhythm with the hop on the upbeat. It can be danced forward LOD or in a single or couple CW turn.

Progression in Duple Minor Contra Dances: In a contra dance, where two couples are working together, the active couples (or #1 couples) progress down the set, and the inactive couples (or #2 couples) progress up the set. A couple, or couples, at the top and bottom of the set are left out of the dance while they change from active to inactive at the bottom and inactive to active at the top. This happens every other time the dance is performed if there is an even number of couples.

Progression in Triple Minor Contra Dances: Three couples' groups work together, with the #1 couple active and #2 and #3 couples inactive. At the end of the first time through the dance figure, the #1 couple has progressed down one position, with #2 moving up the set to become #3. The #3 couple becomes #2. When #1 reaches the bottom of the set, they slide behind the inactive couple down to the very bottom of the set so the progression can continue. The couple left out at the top waits until there are two inactive couples below them to start the figure as #1.

Promenade Position: Couples face the same direction side-by-side, lady on the right, with R. hands joined and L. hands underneath in promenade, or skater position. In a quadrille promenade, the gent holds the hands up and forward, giving a gentlemanly lead to his partner.

Promenade: In the above position, couples walk CCW around the quadrille set or across the contra or quadrille set and back.

Proper: A longways set with all gents on one side or line and ladies on the other, as opposed to **Improper**, where the active couples in a contra dance change places with their partners, forming a lady-gent-lady-gent line on each side.

Quadrille: The quadrille formation is a four-couple square. The popular mid-nineteenth-century quadrille was more sedate than its forerunner, the cotillion. It was elegant and citified with emphasis on proper deportment and manners. Dancers walked in a languid, graceful manner. Show off steps were frowned upon by urban elite as vulgar. It consisted of four or five figures. Each figure was danced to different music often composed in a classical style, using popular opera tunes or arrangements of classical music melodies.

Right and Left (Across and Back in Quadrilles): Couples walk forward, taking R. hands with the person they are facing in the opposite couple, pulling by to take L. hands with partner.

Gent leads the lady around, turning CCW, to take the place of the opposite couple. They return home in the same manner.

Right and Left Through in Contra Dances: Couples walk across the set, passing R. shoulders with the opposite (4). They pivot shoulder to shoulder halfway around CCW, person on the right walks forward, person on the left walks backwards (4) to face across the set. They return in the same manner (16). If the lines are improper, the gent, after the pass through, takes the lady's L. hand in his to lead her halfway around.

Salute: A long slow bow or curtsy.

Schottische: A step danced in a smooth and even 4/4 meter, consisting of running steps and step hops.

Sicilian Circle: A double circle with sets of two couples facing each other. The ladies are on the right of the gents. Couples progress around the circle in the direction they are initially facing, as in The Spanish Waltz. Trios, gent in the middle of two ladies, can also follow this formation, as in Scotch Reel.

Side Couples: This refers to couples #3 and #4 in a quadrille who repeat the same figure the sides have just danced.

Swing: The "**waist swing**," where the couple is turning in closed ballroom position with the gent's R. arm around the lady's waist, was discouraged in Mormon pioneer dances. Instead they were encouraged to dance a Two-Hand Swing, where partners turn together with two hands joined.

Tucker: This refers to an extra gent in a dance who is seeking a partner.

Top of the set: The end of a longways set that is closest to the band and caller.

Top Couple: The couple at the top of a longways set.

Touch: Is a movement of the foot on the floor that does not take weight.

Triple Minor: A contra dance with three couples working together, progressing up and down the set. Couples 1, 4, 7, etc. are active.

Waltz: A dance step in an even 3/4 meter with an accent on the first beat. It consists of three steps danced in a smooth and graceful manner.

Resources

BIBLIOGRAPHY

Arrington, Georganna B. "Dance in Mormonism: the Dancingest Denomination." *Focus on Dance X: Religion and Dance*. AAHPERD, National Dance Association (1982): 31–35.

Aunt Carrie. *Popular Pastimes for Field and Fireside, or Amusements for Young and Old*. Springfield: Milton Bradley & Co., 1867.

Bitton, Davis. "These Licentious Days": Dancing Among the Mormons. *Sunstone Magazine* vol. 2. (1998): 16–27.

Brown, Lois S. "Waltz to the Rescue." *Saga of the Sanpitch* vol. 18. (1986): 4–5.

Burchenal, Elizabeth A. B. *American Country-Dances*. New York, Boston: G. Schirmer, 1918.

———. *Folk-Dances of Denmark*. New York: G. Schirmer, 1915.

Burton, Richard. *City of the Saints, Among the Mormons and Across the Rocky Mountains to California*. New York: Harper and Brothers, 1862.

Cameron, Marguerite. *This Is The Place*. Caldwell: Caxton Printers, 1939.

Carter, Kat. *Treasures of Pioneer History* vol. 2. Salt Lake City: Daughters of Utah Pioneers, 1953.

Cellarius (Pseud.). *Fashionable Dancing.* Memphis: General Books, LLC, 2012. (Scanned re-print. First translated and published in London 1847.)

Czarnowski, Lucille K. *Dances of Early California Days.* Palo Alto: Pacific Books, 1950.

Damon, S. Foster. "The History Of Square Dancing," *Proceedings of the American Antiquarian Society* vol. 62, no. 1. (1952) 62–98.

Daughters of Utah Pioneers. *Pioneer Songs.* Salt Lake City: Utah Printing Co., 1978.

Dick's Quadrille Call-Book. New York: Dick & Fitzgerald, 1878.

Dodworth, Allen. *Dancing and it's Relation to Education and Social Life.* New York and London: Harper & Brothers Publishers, 1900.

Dugan, Anne S., Jeanette Schlottmann, and Abbie Rutledge. *Folk Dances of Scandinavia.* New York: A. S. Barnes and Company, 1948.

Durang, Charles. *The Fashionable Dancers Casket, Ballroom Instructor.* Philadelphia: Fisher & Brothers, 1856. (Scanned re-print. Bedford, MA: Applewood Books, 1996.)

Ferrero, Edward. *The Art of Dancing, Historically Illustrated.* New York: self-published, 1859. (Bibiolife Scanned re-print.)

Ford, Mr. and Mrs. Henry. *"Good Morning!" Music, Calls, and Directions for Old-Time Dancing.* 4th ed. Dearborn: Dearborn Publishing, 1943.

Forsgren, Lydia Walker. "History of Box Elder County," *(unpublished).* Daughters of Utah Pioneers Museum Archives, n.d.

Godfrey, Kenneth W., Audrey M. Godfrey and Jill Mulvay Derr. *Women's Voices, An Untold History of the Latter-Day*

Saints, 1830–1900. Salt Lake City: Deseret Book Company, 1982.

Harris, J., A. Pittman and M. Waller. *Dance A While, Handbook of folk, Square and Social Dance,* 4th ed. Minneapolis: Burgess Publishing Co., 1955.

Hicks, Michael. *Mormonism and Music, A History.* Urbana & Chicago: University of Illinois Press, 2003.

Hillgove, Thomas. *Complete Practical Guide to the Art of Dancing.* New York: Dick & Fitzgerald, 1863.

Hogge, Donna M. "A Study of the Dance in the Church of Jesus Christ of Latter-day Saints." Master's thesis, Utah State University, 1948.

Holbrook, Leona. "Pioneer Dancing." Lesson for May 1981. Salt Lake City: Daughters of Utah Pioneers, 1981.

———. "Dancing As an Aspect of Early Mormon and Utah Culture." *Brigham Young University Studies,* vol. 16. no. 1. (1975): 117–38.

Holden, R., F. Kaltman, and O. Kublitsky. *The Contra Dance Book.* American Squares Dance Series 3. Wilmington, DL, 1956.

Howe, Elias, *American Dancing Master, and Ball-room Prompter, Containing About Five Hundred Dances.* Memphis, TN: General Books, LLC, 2012. (Scanned re-print. First published in 1858.)

Jennings, J. B. "Backward Glance at Dancing," *Improvement Era,* 39, The Church of Jesus Christ of Latter-day Saints, (June 1936): 380–81.

Johnson, Don Carlos, *A Brief History of Springville, Utah.* Springville, Utah: William F. Gibson, 1900.

Kennedy, Douglas, ed. *Community Dance Manual, Books 1–7.* London: The English Folk Dance and Song Society, 1967.

Laufman, Dudley and Jaqueline Laufman. *Traditional Barn Dances with Calls & Fiddling.* Champaign, IL: Human Kinetics, 2008.

Linscott, Eloise Hubbard, ed., *Folk Songs of Old New England.* New York: Dover Publications, Inc., 1993, (replica of 2nd edition 1962, 1939, original edition).

Longden, Sanna. *Historic & Contemporary Dances for Kids & Teachers.* DVD No. 2. FolkStyle Productions. Evanston, IL. 2001, 2004

Longden, Sanna. *More Favorite Folk Dances of Kids & Teachers.* DVD No. 4. FolkStyle Productions.Evanston, IL. 1996, 2004.

Madsen, Susan A. *Christmas, A Joyful Heritage.* Salt Lake City, UT: Deseret Book Company, 1984.

Magriel, Paul, ed. *Chronicles of the American Dance.* New York: Da Capo Press, Inc. 1948.

Marks, Joseph E. III. *America Learns to Dance.* New York: Exposition Press, 1957.

McGavin, Cecil, E. *The Mormon Pioneers.* Salt Lake City, UT: Stevens and Wells, Inc., 1947.

McKinnan, Della, "History of Randolf, UT," (unpublished) Daughters of Utah Pioneers Museum Archives.

Merrill, A. M. "Dancing" (The) *Improvement Era,* 2, (October 1908): 949–52.

Miller, Craig R., *An Old-Time Utah Dance Party, Sheet Music and Dance Steps.* Salt Lake City, UT: Utah Arts Council, 2000.

Miner, Laraine, *Early Utah Dances,* master's thesis, California State University, Hayward CA. 1983.

Morrison, James E., *Twenty Four Early American Country Dances, Cotillions & Reels for the Year 1976.* New York, NY: The Country Dance Society, Inc. 1976.

Neff, Andrew L. *History of Utah 1849–1869.* Salt Lake City: Deseret News Press, 1940.

O'Dea, Thomas F. *The Mormons.* Chicago: University of Chicago Press, 1957.

Page, Ralph. *Heritage Dances of Early America.* Colorado Springs, CO: The Lloyd Shaw Foundation, 1976.

Pugliese, Patri J. *Pugliese's Dances for The Civil War Ballroom, A Manual of Dance Instruction to Accompany The Civil War Ballroom Recording by Spare Parts.* Lanesboro, MA: Stellar Productions. 2011.

Rice, Clayton S. *The Mormon Way.* Salt Lake City, UT: Clayton S. Rice, 1929.

Rohrbough, Lynn, *Handy Play Party Book.* (Original edition 1949 revised by Cecilia Riddwell) Burnsville, North Carolina: World Around Songs, Inc., 1982.

Ryan, Grace L. *Dances of Our Pioneers.* New York: A. S. Barnes & Company, 1926 and 1939.

Shaw, Dorothy. *The Story of Square Dancing,* Los Angeles: Sets in Order, Handbook Series, 1967.

Shaw, Lloyd. *Cowboy Dances.* Caldwell, ID: The Caxton Printers, LTD., 1939.

———. *The Round Dance Book.* Caldwell, ID: The Caxton Printers, LTD., 1948.

Shumway, Larry, "Dancing the Buckles off Their Shoes in Pioneer Utah." *Brigham Young University Studies,* 37, #3, (1997–98) 7–50.

Skidmore, Rex, A. "Mormon Recreation in theory and Practice: A Study of Social Change." PhD diss., University of Pennsylvania, 1941.

Smith, George D., ed., *An Intimate Chronicle, The Journals of William Clayton,* Signature Books in Association with Smith Research Associates, Salt Lake City, 1955, 250.

Smith, Joseph Jr. *History of the Church of Jesus Christ of Latter-day Saints* (Salt Lake City: Deseret Book, 1971).

Smuckler, David and David Millstone. *Cracking Chestnuts, The Living Tradition of Classic American Contra Dances.* Haydenville MA: The Country Dance and Song Society, Inc., 2008.

Stell, Liz, and Bill Matthiesen. *The Civil War Ballroom Band Book, Music for a Midcentury Victorian Ball.* 2005.

Stegner, Wallace. *Mormon Country.* New York: Duell, Sloan, and Pearce, 1942.

Teten, Carol. *A Nineteenth Century Ball: The Charm of Group Dances. How to Dance Through Time Vol. VI.* DVD. Dancetime Publications. Kentfield CA. 2001, 2003.

Tolman, Beth, and Ralph Page. *The Country Dance Book, The Best of the Square and Contra Dances and All About Them.* Brattleboro, VT: The Stephen Greene Press, 1976.

Tolman, Henry & Co., *The Welcome Guest: A Collection of Modern Piano-Forte Music, Being a Choice Repertoire of Pieces for Home Amusement, Comprising the Most Popular Rondos, Nocturnes, Marches, Waltzes, Polkas, Schottisches, Galops, Mazurkas, Redowas, Quadrilles, Cotillions, etc.* New York: S. T. Gordon. 1863.

Tullidge, Edward W. *History of Salt Lake City.* Salt Lake City, UT: Star Publishing Co. 1886.

Walker, Ronald W. and Michael Quinn. "Virtuous, Lovely, or of Good Report, How the Church Has Fostered the Arts." *Ensign of the Church of Jesus Christ of Latter-day Saints*, 7 #7. (July 1977) 81–93.

Wesson, Karl E. "Dance in the Church of Jesus Christ of Latter-day Saints, 1830–1940." Master's thesis, Brigham Young University, 1975.

Williams, Vivian T., ed., *The Beemer Manuscript, Dance Music Collected in the Gold Mining Camp of Warren's Diggins, Idaho in the 1860's*, Seattle, WA: Voyager Recordings & Publications, 2008.

———, *The Haynes Family Manuscript, Pioneer Dance Music from the Willamette Valley of Oregon.* Seattle, WA: Voyager Recordings & Publications, 2010.

Wilson, Marguerite, *Dancing.* Philadelphia: The Penn Publishing Company, 1907.

Wilson, Thomas. *A Companion to the Ball Room, Containing a Choice Collection of Original and Admired Country Dances.* London: D. Mackay, 1820.

Wirth, Professor A. C. *Complete Quadrille Call Book and Dancing Master.* (First published in 1902). Newmarket, NH: A Captain Fiddle Publications Reprint, 2002.

Yashko, Ruth E. "An Historical Study of Pioneer Dancing in Utah." Master's thesis, University of Utah, 1947.

Young, Levi Edgar. *The Founding of Utah.* New York: Charles Scribner's Sons. 1923.

DISCOGRAPHY

Beehive Band, *The Beehive Band, Hymns, Songs, and Fiddle Tunes of the Utah Pioneers.* CD. Honeybee Recordings. 1997.

Carter, Tom, Jan H. Brunvand, and H. Reynolds Cannon. *The New Beehive Songster, Volume I.* Okehdokee Records, Salt Lake City, UT. 1975.

Matthieson, Bill, *The Civil War Ballroom, Music by Spare Parts.* CD. 1997.

———, *The Regency Ballroom, Music by Spare Parts.* CD. 2007.

———, *Returning Heros, More Music for the Civil War Ballroom by Spare Parts.* CD. 2012.

Miller, Craig R. *An Old-Time Utah Dance Party, Field Recordings of Social Dance Music from the Mormon West.* Two disc set. Utah Arts Council. Salt Lake City, UT. 2000.

Miner, Laraine, *Old Time Utah Dances. Buckle Busters & Pattie Richards.* CD. Salt Lake City, UT. 1995.

Webster, Cory. *They Think We Live on Carrots Down in Utah. Old Pioneer Melodies, Dance Tunes, and Songs.* Buckle Busters. Audio cassette. 1995.

Williams, Vivian, and Phil, *Dance Music of the Oregon Trail.* CD. Voyager Recordings, Seattle WA. 2000.

———. *Fiddle Tunes of the Lewis and Clark Era, A Project in Celebration of the Lewis and Clark Bicentennial.* CD. The New Columbia Fiddlers. Voyager Recordings, Seattle WA. 2002.

———. *Pioneer Dance Tunes of the Far West.* CD. Voyager Recordings, Seattle WA. 2006.

———. *Tunes from The Haynes Family Manuscript, Pioneer Dance Music from the Willamette Valley of Oregon.* CD. Voyager Recordings. Seattle, WA 2011.

———. *Tunes from The Peter Beemer Manuscript. Dance Music from and 1860's Idaho Mining Camp.* CD. Voyager Recordings. Seattle, WA 2009.

Author

LARAINE MINER was born into a family with extensive Mormon pioneer ancestry and a strong music and dance tradition. Her love of folk music and dance was augmented by her participation in the BYU International Folkdance Ensemble and their first European tour in 1964. Since then, she has been avidly researching, teaching, and presenting the traditional folk and social dances of her Mormon pioneer ancestors.

Online Content

Accompanying music tracks available at booksandthings.com.

To claim free music tracks, use download code: QUADRILLE

Scan to visit

www.laraineminer.com